Also by George Schwimmer PhD

Doppelgänger: The Legend Of Lee Harvey Oswald
The Search For David
Adventures In Consciousness
Kicking Cancer Naturally
Distant Healing
Healing Secrets of the Shamans of Mu
Robert Monroe's Altered States
DAVID: leaves from the journal of a soul (ed.)
Muzungu Wendy (ed.)
MU: The First Great Civilization
A. R. MARTIN: Pioneer In Past Life Regression
My Past Lives And Life Plan
The Littlest Soul
PLAYS:
Mystic
Hamlet Dead
O: The Legend of Lee Harvey Oswald

MURDER IN DALLAS

November 22-24, 1963

WHAT REALLY HAPPENED

George Schwimmer PhD

Phoenix 11 Productions
Santa Fe, New Mexico

Edition 1a, June 22, 2023.

Book and cover design by George Schwimmer PhD.

The quotation in the dedication comes from JFK's Inaugural Speech.

Manufactured in the United States of America.

Dedicated to

John Fitzgerald Kennedy

Now the trumpet summons us again—not as a call to battle, though embattled we are. . .but a call to bear the burden of a long twilight struggle. . . .

For murder, though it have no tongue, will speak with most miraculous organ.

Hamlet
William Shakespeare

Contents

Preface

It is estimated that over 2,000 books have been written about the assassination of President John Fitzgerald Kennedy. One bibliography lists over 1,400 titles. I wrote one of those books. So, why another one?

Let's go back in time. Like virtually everyone over the age of three on November 22, 1963, I remember where I was when I heard the news. I can show you within thirty-six inches where I stood on a sidewalk in Jacksonville, Illinois.

At that time I was a thirty-two-year-old theatre director and instructor of theatre at a small Illinois college, heading for my one o'clock class, when a senior student, a young man named John, ran up behind me and breathlessly blurted out, "President Kennedy has been shot, Mr. Schwimmer." I couldn't believe it. However, when I arrived at the staff office, I found the other three members of my department huddled around a radio with serious faces, listening to that tragic news.

The next four days were a nightmare. I and my wife Veronica remained immobile in front of our TV set, only leaving to catch some sleep each night. We ate our meals there. My daughter Krista was only three and a half then but still remembers her parents watching the TV for four days straight. She knew something bad had happened. The world had just turned upside down and never again would be the same, although I didn't know it just then.

I don't recall anything about Lee Harvey Oswald from that time, except that I saw Jack Ruby shoot him on live TV. I watched JFK's funeral – it broke my heart to see JFK's just-three-years-old son John-John salute his dead father's casket. It was all too much. I couldn't deal with the shock. It felt like a family member had been murdered.

I hadn't been very interested in politics and government earlier but had been pleased with JFK's election and performance as president, including his delightful Friday press conferences, his almost poetic speeches, how he handled himself in office and his beautiful family. Now, he was gone, and I had to move on with my life.

Afterwards I really didn't want to read about the assassination – I remember only two books from the next few years, Mark Lane's *Rush to Judgment* (1966), and Josiah Thompson's *Six Seconds in Dallas* (1967) – and there were too many things in my life to contend with, which included starting a career as a theatre director and helping to raise three children. I put the assassination behind me.

There it rested for the next forty-three years. In 2006 I gave my few Kennedy books to a friend. Let the dead bury the dead. JFK's death now existed in another life for me. Or so I thought. Plus, a new chapter had opened up for me – I began to write: books, screenplays and stage plays.

In the fall of 2009 I started work on a screenplay in which I mentioned Lee Harvey Oswald. I decided to look into the JFK assassination to see if there was anything I could use in my script. I read two or three books and began to feel disturbed. Much of the information about Oswald was quite confusing, didn't make sense. I kept reading, until it dawned on me that Oswald had been right – he *was* a patsy, he *had* been set up, and the assassination *was* a conspiracy, a coup d'etat. And not only had three men been shot to death in Dallas in three days, but Oswald had been falsely branded a mad killer, among other false accusations.

I was shocked by many of the things I eventually discovered – you will be too. And the idea that the President of the United States, the Chief Justice of the U.S. Supreme Court, the FBI, the CIA, Dallas police and others in government could be involved in JFK's assassination and/or its cover-up – and then 'frame' an innocent man for the murder and kill him – seemed inconceivable, bordering on the bizarre, a bad B movie. Yet that's exactly what happened, and so what trust I then had in the federal government disappeared – never to return. How could it? To this day our government is hiding the truth – now carried out by men who weren't even born when JFK died. How can such Americans keep covering up premeditated murder and conspiracy? That's the stuff of dictatorships.

Yet I did not consider writing a book about JFK's assassination or Oswald. I had more than enough writing lined up. All the same, I felt an obligation to JFK, LHO and my country – no justice had been provided for them, and probably never would be – but at least some of the truth needed to come out.

I began serious research of Oswald's life. My logic was simple: if Oswald did not kill JFK and police officer J. D. Tippit, then there had to be a conspiracy. Six years later I self-published *DOPPELGÄNGER: The Legend Of Lee Harvey Oswald*, which I believe clearly demonstrates my thesis. I thought I was done. Little did I know. Because for the next six years I kept stumbling across more assassination material and kept adding it to my book. I knew I was in the grip of "researcher's disease," which has consumed many a prospective Ph.D. candidate who can't stop his research and write his dissertation. At least I had written my book.

Finally, at the start of 2022, I felt I could end the search. Nothing of great interest to me had emerged in the past couple of years, but then. . .I kept noticing some facts published only in two or three books but not elsewhere. Same with other facts, in other books. All having to do with what had taken place in Dallas on those three tragic days. Why hadn't someone pulled all these facts together in one volume?

In addition, many of the best JFK assassination books were long out of print, and sellers often were asking outrageous prices for used copies. Further, Jim Marr's *Crossfire* is 612 pages long, David Lifton's *Best Evidence* is 747 pages, and John Armstrong's *Harvey and Lee* is over 1,000 pages (with 750-800 words per page). Who would take on these books today? Only those seriously interested.

Then how many people under fifty are aware of the most significant JFK assassination facts uncovered by thousands of citizen researchers since November 1963? Not many. It's taken me thirteen years to accumulate the contents of this book, culled from many sources. As a former college professor, I know that my job is to find every fact I can, pull out the strongest of those facts, and make as powerful a case for a conspiracy as possible.

I also want to put you the reader in the shoes of the individuals I've written about, so that you get a sense of their experiences. So, in this narrative the facts tell a story, and a very strange and disturbing story you will find it to be.

This book, *though it have no tongue, will speak with most miraculous organ* about the death of John Fitzgerald Kennedy.

Introduction

Three Dallas murders:

President John Fitzgerald Kennedy,

Police officer J. D. Tippit,

ONI/CIA agent 'Lee Harvey Oswald.'

These deaths rocked the United States and the world from November 22, 1963 at 12:30:47 P.M. and 1:06 P.M. (CST), until November 24, 1963 at 11:21 A.M. – forever changing the course of history, for the worse, much worse, as we all discovered to our dismay during subsequent years.

DOPPELGÄNGER: The Legend Of Lee Harvey Oswald, establishes – by the overwhelming preponderance of evidence – that there were two men who used the name Lee Harvey Oswald for at least eleven years, that both had been recruited, trained and employed by the Office of Naval Intelligence (ONI) and the Central Intelligence Agency (CIA),[1] that 'Harvey' had impersonated Lee for all those years, while Lee had impersonated 'Harvey' in 1963, and that the man who Jack Ruby had shot to death had

'Lee Harvey Oswald'

Passport photo: Lee.   Booking photo: 'Harvey'.

Notice the ear at left is larger and set higher on the head, and the neck at left is wider. Eye at right is deep-set.

been 'Harvey.' In addition, 'Harvey's' innocence and Lee's guilt in the tragedy are clearly revealed.

So, *DOPPELGÄNGER's* principal focus is on 'Harvey Oswald,' not on other facts (real, manipulated, suppressed or false) available from the Warren Commission (WC) files, witness statements, testimonies, depositions, Dallas Police Department (DPD) reports, FBI reports, hard evidence and so on. There are areas of assassination inquiry that are barely touched on in *DOPPELGÄNGER*.

It finally became obvious, however, that no book about the Kennedy tragedy had focused *just* on the events, participants and evidence *in Dallas* during those three days. This narrative consequently attempts to present as many truthful, accurate and complete details about the events and individuals of November 22-24 identified to date, in order to put the reader on ground level of the fifty-seven hours whose focus this book is.

Surprisingly, there is more, rather than less, evidence available from witnesses; consequently only the most relevant, striking, logical and verifiable accounts have been chosen for this book, again employing the principle of preponderance of evidence. So, since more often than not there are anomalies in witness reports, if, for example, four witnesses agree on the colors and cut of a suspect's clothing and two others give diverging descriptions, only what the four reported will be given in this book. It is pointless to include the chaff with the wheat.

Further, as there was extensive lying by members of the DPD, FBI, etc., and since no known tape recordings or stenographic records of 'Harvey's' interrogations were made, primarily the statements made by 'Harvey' himself – and recorded by print and broadcast journalists and cameramen – will be used. 'Harvey' had a stiff and formal manner of speaking – almost like a foreigner – and did not use slang and idioms. So, for example, when *supposedly* asked by a detective why he *supposedly* brought a handgun to the Texas Theatre, 'Harvey's' *supposed* reply, "You know how boys do when they have a gun, they carry it," is simply unbelievable. It also is likely that at times 'Harvey' was not truthful himself, in order to protect his role as a deep cover intelligence operative.

Because of the tight focus on 'Harvey' in *DOPPELGÄNGER*, a few pieces of information from that book, here encapsulated, must be mentioned:

1. the recruitment of 'Harvey' – apparently a Hungarian immigrant living in New York City's "Little Hungary," who spoke fluent Russian and who probably was a year younger than Lee Oswald – at about the age of eleven, most likely by the ONI;

2. 'Harvey's' training as a false defector and spy by the ONI and CIA, who for years groomed him for his role, which included supplying him with a bogus 'mother,' 'Marguerite Oswald;'

3. the substitution of 'Harvey' for Lee that occurred in the fall of 1958, when Marine 'Harvey' went to the Marine Corps Air Facility in Tustin, California, in place of Lee. 'Harvey' was assigned there from October, 1958, until his discharge in September, 1959,[2] while Lee, also in the Marine Corps, in early 1959 went to the Army's Monterey, California language school, where he became fluent in Spanish;

4. 'Harvey's' legitimate and faithful service to the CIA from the time he was recruited until he went to New Orleans on April 24, 1961, after which he was co-opted by rogue CIA operatives, pulled into the assassination plot by Clay Shaw, and set up to be the patsy for the JFK murder, probably by CIA's David Atlee Phillips;

5. 'Harvey's' marriage in Minsk to Marina Prusacova in 1961 and the birth of their first daughter, June, in 1962;

6. 'Harvey's' New Orleans love affair in the spring and summer of 1963 with Judyth Vary Baker;

7. 'Harvey's' meeting in Dallas, early in September, 1963, while still in New Orleans, with his CIA handler, David Atlee Philips, a.k.a. 'Maurice Bishop,' who from '61 to '63 had been the CIA's Chief of Covert Action in Mexico City. He introduced Harvey to Antonio Veciana, who had left Cuba in '61 and formed Alpha 66, a powerful anti-Castro group (funded by the CIA and overseen by Phillips);

8. 'Harvey's' *actual* trip to Mexico City to deliver a deadly strain of cancer cells to an agent from Cuba, versus the CIA-invented Mexico City trip by 'Lee Harvey Oswald' (Lee Oswald and at least two other impersonators), during which time 'Oswald' supposedly visited the Cuban Consulate and the Soviet Embassy;

9. that Lee Oswald worked in Jack Ruby's Carousel Club during the summer of 1963 and was seen there by many individuals.

It also has to be understood that *high level rogue CIA operatives* planned, organized and supervised the assassination, and that they used the CIA's most prized tools: secrecy, deception and – especially – confusion, which included the doppelgänger 'Lee Harvey Oswalds' and other 'Oswald' impersonators. Also crucial to the success of the operation was the CIA's "need to know" policy, which in effect put each element of the plot in its own little information bubble, so that each person or small group knew only what they themselves would do and knew only those other participants in their own information bubble.

For example, there were two groups of assassins and two individual assassins in Dealey Plaza on November 22, but there is little likelihood that any knew who the others were, or how many, or where they were positioned. Overlying all this was the CIA's "plausible deniability," which the plotters used to hide their treachery.

As Texas journalist Jim Marrs pointed out in his book *Crossfire*, "No one single matter of fact in this case can be accepted uncritically. Evidence of deceit, misrepresentation and manipulation abounds. The very people charged with finding the truth engaged in fabrication, alteration, suppression of evidence, as well as intimidation of witnesses."[3] Not to mention the later murders of some who knew too much. And understand very clearly that what happened in Dallas was premeditated murder, insurrection and treason, in which many individuals took part.

The pivotal figure in the following narrative is designated 'Harvey' for three reasons: 1) for a year, around age twelve, this individual had called *himself* 'Harvey,' 2) almost two dozen references to "Harvey Lee Oswald" have been found in various intelligence files by researchers, and 3) to differentiate 'Harvey' from Lee, and because it is obvious that the name "Harvey Lee Oswald" was used by the intelligence community to keep 'Harvey' Oswald documents separate from Lee Oswald documents.

This book presents to a new generation what really happened in Dallas on November 22-24, 1963 and once and for all demolishes the ridiculous claim of "a lone nut" with an antiquated Italian carbine, three shots and "the magic bullet." History, the American people, John Kennedy and 'Harvey Oswald' deserve no less.[4]

The ultimate goal of the following narrative, however, is to help excise the malignancy that has grown unchecked

13

on the spirit of the United States since JFK's death. Although the origins and cause of this malignancy have been rigidly kept secret by the government and major media, in recent years the malignancy has broken into plain sight, revealing that it has spread from the highest to the lowest levels of society and threatens our very democracy.

Both Sophocles' *Oedipus* and Shakespeare's *Hamlet* reveal how the moral stench of the hidden murder of a leader soon rises from beneath the folds of lies covering it and sickens – by both physical and moral plagues – all under its sway, in this case the entire world, since the course of world history was severely altered by the murder of John Fitzgerald Kennedy.

It is time now to rip away the folds of lies covering the Kennedy murder and reveal what actually took place on November 22, so that real healing may finally start to take place.

Prelude

A PREPERATORY MURDER

Thomas B. Shipman

October 14, 1963

Secret Service agent Tom Shipman was one of three agents who regularly drove President Kennedy's limousine. On this day, he had been in Camp David, had eaten lunch, then had told others he wasn't feeling well. He went to take a nap, during which he suffered a fatal 'heart attack.' No autopsy or toxicology tests were performed, and his death certificate is still unavailable. He had received a clean bill of health on his annual physical a month earlier. He was only 51. His wife was urged to bury him quickly, and he was laid in the ground two days later.

Shipman previously had learned he would be working in Dallas on November 22. He had planned to have dinner that evening with his sister-in-law, a Dallas resident. In a phone call to her he said he was concerned about the

President's safety and would take any action to protect JFK. Strangely, Shipman once had told family that he thought JFK would be killed one day.

A dozen years after Shipman's death, the CIA revealed that some time back it had developed an undetectable poison which would bring on a 'heart attack.' A Secret Service agent later gave a statement to a researcher that Shipman had been murdered.[1]

Shipman's callous death in effect helped to change the course of world history, like the "butterfly effect," for it opened the door to Secret Service agent William Greer being JFK's November 22 limousine driver.

RUBY, TIPPIT, WHITE
November 14, 1963

In the evening, a witness saw long-time mobster Jack Ruby with DPD Officer J. D. Tippit in Ruby's Carousel Club (1312½ Commerce Street, eight blocks southeast of the TSBD), along with a third man, Bernard Weissman. The three talked for more than two hours. Jack's sister, Eva Grant, later told the *New York Herald Tribune* that both she and Jack knew Tippit, that "Tippit used to come into [Jack's] Vegas Club and Carousel Club," and that Jack "called him 'buddy.'" At least six witnesses, including

Dallas Police Lieutenant George C. Arnett, confirmed that Jack Ruby knew Tippit.

Robert "Tosh" Plumlee, then a CIA contract pilot, has written that J. D. Tippit and Roscoe White (another member of the DPD) were part of a special DPD tactical team that would operate in support of U.S. intelligence operations, especially the 112th Military Intelligence Group, which worked with the ONI.

White, who was hired by the DPD only on October 7, 1963 as a clerk-photographer, had been a Marine, and had been on the U.S.S. Bexar at the same time as Lee Oswald when both had shipped out to Japan. White may have been an intelligence operative, black ops, going back to his Marine days. His wife, Geneva, was a dancer at Ruby's Carousel Club, and White was said to know Jack Ruby well.

THE SHOOTERS GATHER

Although many candidates have been put forward as the killers of President Kennedy, the following men are most likely to have been the assassins:

Corsican Hit Men

c. November 15, 1963

Imprisoned French drug smuggler Christian David many years later told researcher Steve Rivele that three

Corsican assassins from Marseille, one of them Lucien Sarti, had shot JFK. Sarti was known to be a very reckless assassin and to wear disguises like a police uniform or a military uniform.

The men had been flown to Mexico, where they stayed in Mexico City for three or four weeks, then crossed the U.S. border at Brownsville, Texas. There they were met by a representative of the Chicago Mafia and driven to a "safe house" in Dallas. For the next few days they took photographs of Dealey Plaza and studied them.

It was decided, Christian David said, that one shooter would be stationed in front of JFK, while the other two would be behind him, "one high and one low (almost horizontal)."[2]

James Files

November 15, 1963

James Files, then 21, many years later stated that while in the Army he had been recruited into CIA operations by the CIA's David Atlee Phillips – that Phillips was his control.

He had driven to Texas a week before the assassination and had stayed at a motel in Mesquite, fourteen miles east of Dallas. Files: "The following day, Lee Harvey Oswald came by [driving a green truck similar to one owned by

18

Jack Ruby]. . .and he took me out to. . .somewhere southeast of Mesquite, where I test fired the weapons and calibrated the scopes. Then he was with me for a few days in town there [Dallas]. We drove around. . .so I would know all the streets."[3] That was Lee Oswald, of course – Harvey couldn't have been with Files. Earline Roberts, Harvey's housekeeper, later testified Harvey was in his room all that weekend, and he was at work every day the next week. Further, as noted earlier, Lee had worked for Ruby the previous summer, during which time he drove the green truck to Ruby's mechanic on more than one occasion.

Operation 40

November 19, 1963

Operation 40, a top secret CIA project, received its name because originally it included 40 fighters. It was later increased to 70 fighters. The group was presided over by Vice President Richard Nixon, and CIA's Tracy Barnes became the operating officer. The first meeting, chaired by Barnes, took place on January 18, 1960 and was attended by David Atlee Phillips, E. Howard Hunt and two other CIA officers. So Phillips and Hunt had an almost four year association with Operation 40 before JFK's death. That year, 1960, Nixon recruited an "important group of businessmen, headed by George H. W. Bush and Jack

Crichton, both Texas oilmen, to gather the necessary funds for the operation."[4]

The fighters, mostly Cuban exiles, were stationed in Miami and focused on anti-Castro projects, which included training in the Everglades for guerrilla warfare aimed at toppling the Castro regime. Some of the recruits were specially instructed to carry out assassinations. One fighter, Marita Lorenz, later said she trained with [Lee] Oswald and knew him as "Ozzie." She didn't like him, thought he was "a creep."[5] Other members of the group were Gerry Patrick Hemming (a former Marine who had lent help to Castro) and Frank Sturgis (Fiorini), who was trained in guerilla tactics and gathering intelligence in World War II and also served in the Cuban revolution.

Two carloads of Operation 40 agents, including Lorenz, Sturgis and Hemming, left Miami for Dallas on the morning of November 19. In the trunks of the cars were many weapons, one of which was Sturgis' rifle, which had a scope and silencer. They drove for two days, rotating drivers. Sturgis was in charge of the group and wouldn't tell Lorenz what their assignment in Dallas was.[6]

Malcolm "Mac" Wallace
November 21, 1963

Wallace was reputedly Lyndon B. Johnson's hit man.

Roger Stone has stated that, "Wallace was the shooter from the 6th floor of the Texas School Book Depository (TSBD). He left a perfect match fingerprint on a box in the "sniper nest," a place he had no reason to be. Six eyewitnesses [saw] a man on the 6th floor who met the description of Mac Wallace. He was an ex-Marine marksman and a convicted murderer, and I can tie him irrevocably to [Lyndon] Johnson."[7]

The only logical reason for Wallace to have been a shooter – if he was – would have been to link him to and consequently implicate and control LBJ. Conceivably Wallace himself might have been coerced into being a shooter.

THE ENABLERS

November 22, 1963

More than thirty enablers are thought to have been in and around Dealey Plaza on November 22. The following are those known to have had roles:

1. Two or more spotters for the shooters.
2. One "railway worker" who spirited away a rifle.
3. "Umbrella Man" and "Radio Man."
4. At least two getaway drivers.
5. A trophy photographer.
6. Jack Ruby.

7. In the assassination headquarters (which must have been close to Dealey Plaza), an unknown number of men, including a radio expert. David Atlee Phillips and E. Howard Hunt may have been there, as they later admitted being in Dallas on November 22.

8. Four or more Secret Service agents.

9. At least seven false 'Secret Service agents' in Dealey Plaza.

10. Chauncey Holt, a criminal who worked for the CIA and who forged fifteen false 'Secret Service' credentials that were used in Dealey Plaza on November 22. He also later claimed to have been one of the "three tramps" arrested on November 22 and to have forged documents in the names of "Lee Harvey Oswald" and "A. J. Hidell," most likely for the CIA.

11. Dallas County Sheriff Bill Decker.

12. Dallas motorcycle police officer Marion L. Baker.

13. False 'policemen' in back of the picket fence and on "the grassy knoll."

14. Nine Texas School Book Depository employees, two or three with foreknowledge, two or three participating, the rest covering up.

MISSING, ALTERED, DISAPPEARED, BOGUS

In order to carry out the JFK assassination, it was

imperative that:

- certain actions be taken;
- certain actions not be taken;
- certain arrangements be made;
- evidence be made to disappear;
- evidence be altered;
- false evidence and false facts be created;
- witnesses be suppressed or ignored.

For example, members of the 112th Army Intelligence Group at Fort Sam Houston had been trained specifically to help the Secret Service protect the President on his travels around the U.S. In the recent (1963) JFK trips, the unit always had carried out its protective duties. Not this time. The unit was preparing to deploy to Dallas, when it was ordered to stand down. Commanding Officer Maximilian Reich protested strongly but was firmly told not to bring his troops to Dallas, depriving JFK of the unit's protection.[9] It is unknown who gave the order, but the Secret Service had the final say. As this narrative progresses, other such manipulations will be seen.

THE ABORT TEAM

William Robert "Tosh" Plumlee

November 20-22, 1963

CIA contract pilot "Tosh" Plumlee was assigned as

23

copilot for a top secret flight which was attached to a Military Intelligence unit and supported by the CIA. The mission: to abort an attempt on the President's life in Dallas, Texas. The CIA's knowledge of the assassination attempt had been obtained from Texas informants and international sources, then passed on to Military Intel units attached to the Pentagon, Plumlee later wrote.

The pre-mission briefing was held at Loxahatchee, Florida the evening of November 20th. The team was instructed where to go, what to look for, how to abort. They would be looking for a minimum of twenty people in Dallas' Dealey Plaza; however, most team members felt this was a false alarm, according to Plumlee. Since Plumlee was only copilot, most of the details of the operation were given to him only after the group was airborne.

The first leg of the flight was from Lantana, Florida (south of West Palm Beach) to Tampa. The group took off before daybreak on the 21st, expecting to arrive in Tampa about sunup. Changing planes in Tampa, they continued on to New Orleans, then to Houston International Airport, where they spent the night.

AN UNLIKELY HERALD

Rose Cherami

November 20, 1963

Cherami, a.k.a. Melba Christine Marcades and 35 other aliases, was a prostitute, heroin addict and drug runner. On this night, she was on her way from Florida to Dallas – where she had previously worked as an exotic dancer in Jack Ruby's Carousel Club – when, she claimed, she was thrown from a moving car in which she had been riding with two men. She was brought to Moosa Hospital in Eunice, Louisiana and evaluated, found to have only minor injuries.

However, since she was believed to be a drug addict under the influence and in "severe narcotic withdrawal," the Louisiana State Police were called to take her to East Louisiana State Hospital for withdrawal treatment. On the way there, when the state trooper asked Cherami why she had been traveling to Dallas, she told him, "To, number one, pick up some money, pick up [my] baby, and to kill Kennedy."[10] The trooper did not take her seriously. He should have.

At the hospital, she once again said, this time to hospital staff, that JFK would soon be killed in Dallas.

ENTER THE PLAYERS
Wednesday, November 20
8:00 A.M. [11]

Harvey Oswald reported for work as usual at the Texas

25

School Book Depository (TSBD), where he had been hired on October 15 by TSBD superintendent Roy S. Truly, who had been advised that Harvey was an FBI informant.[12] As with Harvey's two previous jobs, this one had been arranged for him by his renegade CIA handlers. He worked 5 days a week, 40 hours, 45 minutes for lunch, was paid $1.25 an hour, filling book orders in the large TSBD warehouse. His foreman was William H. Shelley, who later claimed to have worked for the CIA. In addition, Shelley was arrested in 1960 for weapons theft.[13] Harvey's co-worker Billy Lovelady was charged with handling stolen pistols in January, 1963[14], and Black co-worker Charles Givens had a police record involving narcotics.

The TSBD company only procured its seven-story building at 411 Elm Street a year before the assassination, substantially renovated it, and moved in sometime during the summer of 1963.[15]

In November, 1963, the building had three elevators. There was a passenger elevator near the southeast corner, which only went up to the fourth floor. In the northwest corner were a flight of steps going to the seventh floor, which employees were told not to use, as the steps needed repair. East of the staircase, against the north wall, were two freight elevators. One of these, the west elevator, had a gate that had to be lowered for the elevator to function. When the gate was down, this elevator could be summoned from another floor. The east elevator did not have a gate and could not be summoned.

The building, at the corner of Houston Street, was owned by Dallas oilman David Harold Byrd, cousin of conservative U.S. Senator Harry F. Byrd. D. H. Byrd had a close relationship with both Lyndon Johnson and Texas Governor John Connally, was an oil associate of Sid Richardson and Clint Murchison and may have known David Atlee Phillips through the Dallas Petroleum Club, of which George H. W. Bush also was a member.[16]

In November, 1963, Byrd had teamed up with his Ling-Temco-Vought (LTV) partner James Ling to buy 132,000 shares of LTV stock. Although required by SEC rules to report this insider purchase, they delayed doing so until well-past JFK's assassination. After Johnson became President, LTV, which manufactured aircraft, received a large defense contract – in January, 1964 – to build fighter planes for Vietnam.[17] So D. H. Byrd appears to have been well-compensated for the use of his building in the assassination.

Carolyn Arnold, secretary of TSBD V. P. Ochus C. Campbell, said in 1994 that "there is a whole lot more to tell about the TSBD – that the whole building should be suspected…of [being] a 'safe base' to operate from that day in November 1963." [18]

Time unknown

The presidential motorcade route was changed from driving straight down Main Street and onto the Stemmons Freeway to turning right on Houston Street from Main, then left on Elm Street. It's never been clear who ordered the change, but the choice of route was the responsibility of the Secret Service, and no one could overrule its decision, not even the President.

This new route violated Secret Service rules that a presidential motorcade must travel at 44 mph and make no turns of more than 90 degrees. The southwest corner of Elm and Houston Streets was a 120 degree turn, forcing the motorcade to slow to about 11 mph as it turned onto Elm. In addition, the stretch of Elm from Houston to the overpass was a perfect crossfire ambush site: four tall buildings in the rear, four shooting sites in the front.

Prior to a presidential motorcade, buildings are inspected, windows are sealed, sharpshooters are later placed onto some buildings – all Secret Service responsibilities. None of this was done in Dallas for November 22, 1963.

9:00 – 10:00 A.M.

Police officer J. D. Tippit was having coffee at the Dobbs House Restaurant, 1221 N. Beckley (southwest corner of Beckley and Colorado), in Oak Cliff, two blocks north of Harvey's rooming house on Beckley – "*as was his habit about that time most mornings*,"[19] waitress Mary Dowling later said – when another man, also a regular customer, started complaining loudly about his order of eggs. Tippit glanced twice at the man but said nothing. The man was Lee Oswald, impersonating Harvey, and he may have given this performance to help Tippit recognize doppelgänger Harvey (or Lee) in Oak Cliff two days later.

Dowling's statement that Tippit was in the restaurant, "as was his habit about the same time most mornings," is very curious. Dobbs House was *just over six miles* northwest from *the closest point* of Tippit's assigned patrol district, #78. Under normal driving conditions, it would have taken Tippit about forty-five minutes round trip from his assigned district to Dobbs House. Why would he come there for a coffee break "*most mornings*"?

The noisy customer was later identified by the owner and employees as "Lee Harvey Oswald." Waitress Dowling reported that "Oswald" had *usually eaten breakfast* at the restaurant between 7:00 and 7:30 A.M. *(But Harvey's wife*

29

Marina testified that Harvey never ate breakfast – he didn't like to eat in the morning! And Harvey couldn't afford to eat in a restaurant every morning.) Apparently Lee lived just a few blocks from Harvey's rooming house, thus helping to confuse the 'Oswald' record.

Dowling recalled that 'Oswald' was last seen by her in the restaurant that morning at about 10:00 A.M., at which time he was "nasty" and used curse words, like other 'Oswald' impersonators had during the two previous months, to depict 'Oswald' as an obnoxious person. Since Harvey came to work at 8:00 A.M. every morning, it wasn't him.

"Tosh" Plumlee later wrote that there was "an Oak Cliff safe house on North Beckley Street run by Alpha 66's Hernandez group, which had worked out of Miami prior to the assassination." So then, all the 'Oswald' sightings in Oak Cliff would indicate that Lee Oswald had lived at that "safe house" for a while before the assassination. Incidentally, Alpha 66's move from Miami to Dallas seems quite odd. Why would they move to Dallas, and why just then? They had their own "safe house" in Dallas.

Plumlee also wrote that he had met Lee Harvey Oswald on a number of occasions connected with intelligence training in the past, including at Illusionary Warfare

30

Training in Nagshead, North Carolina, in Honolulu at a radar installation, and in Dallas at the Oak Cliff safe house.[20] That 'Oswald' only could have been Lee.

Mid-morning

Two police officers on patrol in Dealey Plaza noticed several men standing behind the picket fence on the "grassy knoll." The men apparently were dry firing, aiming rifles in the direction of the plaza. The policemen immediately headed for the fence, but when they got there, the men were gone, having driven off.[21] It's interesting that there were "several" men and "rifles."

The officers filed a report with the FBI – two days *after* the assassination. The report soon vanished, not to resurface until 1978.

10:30 A.M.

Ralph Leon Yates, a refrigeration mechanic, was driving his pickup truck on the Thornton Expressway when he noticed a man hitchhiking in Oak Cliff near the Beckley Avenue onramp. Yates decided to pick him up.

When the hitchhiker got into the truck, he was carrying "a package about 4 feet to 4 1/2 feet long," covered with brown wrapping paper. Yates told him he could put the package in the back of the pickup, but the man replied that the package contained curtain rods and he'd rather keep it in the cab. The hitchhiker, Yates later said, looked so much like Lee Harvey Oswald that he was in effect Oswald's double.[22]

Yates mentioned to 'Oswald' that people were getting excited about the President's upcoming visit, and 'Oswald' then asked Yates "if he thought a person could assassinate the President" with a rifle from the top of a building or out of a window, high up. He showed Yates a photo of a man holding a rifle.[23] 'Oswald' also asked if Yates thought the President might change his parade route. Yates dropped 'Oswald' off at the stoplight by Elm and Houston Streets and last saw 'Oswald' carrying his package of "curtain rods" over to the TSBD side of Elm Street.[24]

After Yates saw pictures of Harvey in the media, he said the man he gave the ride to was "identical with Oswald." *That* 'Oswald's' comments were – like the behavior of other 'Oswalds' in the self-incriminating incidents already seen – a blatant attempt to draw attention to 'Lee Harvey Oswald' as a potential presidential assassin. This obviously was the same 'Oswald' (Lee) who was in the Dobbs House Restaurant – someone must have picked him up in a car after his explosive display, driven him to the freeway and handed him the "curtain rods" package. Harvey was at work then.

Evening

During the first week of November, 'Lee Harvey Oswald' took a tie, a white shirt and a pair of black trousers for dry cleaning to Gray's Cleaners, 1209 Eldorado Avenue (less than a block west of Harvey's rooming house).[25] Owner and manager Leslie Lawson said he also had seen 'Oswald' on several occasions in August at Reno's Speed Wash, which was next door to Gray's. A former Reno's employee, Joseph Johnson, told the FBI that on the evening of November 20 or 21 "Lee Harvey Oswald" was washing laundry at Reno's and remained there until midnight, reading magazines.

However, Harvey couldn't afford dry cleaners and laundromats on his meager salary – Marina washed all his clothes by hand. Also, both Marina and friend Ruth Paine said that none of Harvey's clothes were ever sent for dry cleaning, and he had absolutely no use for a tie, white shirt and black dress pants while working at the TSBD. Finally, Harvey was in his room on the evening of November 20, and he was in Irving on the evening of November 21. The sightings of 'Oswald' in Gray's and Reno's were of Lee Oswald.

11:00 P.M.

Harvey called his New Orleans lover Judyth,[26] who at

the time was living in Gainesville, Florida. They had kept in touch by phone during the past seven weeks, and Harvey now said that the JFK ambush would occur on Friday afternoon, but he didn't give any details, since that would have put Judyth's life in danger. Earlier, on October 19, Harvey' birthday, he had told Judyth he was spending evenings with men plotting JFK's death and had been invited to take part in the assassination plans. He expected to be killed by the plotters and had said to Judyth, "I won't live to see another birthday cake."[27]

Now he told her that an "abort" team had been called in to help him and would try to intervene in the assassination attempt.[28] Then, "Tomorrow, I'll go say goodbye to Junie and Rachel [born October 20].... My [CIA] handler Phillips is...the traitor.... Remember that name..., David Atlee Phillips."[29] As Harvey ended their conversation, Judyth called him by his "real name," she later wrote.[30] Harvey never spoke with Judyth again. She has never revealed that "real name."

Harvey had been asked to be a shooter he had told Judyth, so it can be assumed that the plotters had wanted him in the TSBD sixth-floor "sniper's nest," not only set up to be the patsy but – as will be seen further on – slated to be gunned down, like he had predicted.

34

Night

The Operation 40 group arrived in Dallas, drove to a motel, registered as a hunting party and brought their weapons from the cars into their two rooms. Sturgis still would not tell Lorenz why they were in Dallas, but she assumed they were there to kill someone.

Sometime after midnight, "Eduardo" (CIA's E. Howard Hunt) arrived, gave Sturgis a large envelope full of money, to be distributed to all present. Hunt was there for about an hour. Then, around 2:00 A.M., a man whom Lorenz later identified as Jack Ruby showed up. Ruby was immediately incensed, stating that he did not do business with "broads." Marita had had enough – "Screw this mission," she said, "I'm going home." Sturgis drove her, and Gerry Heming, to the Dallas airport. They flew back to Miami together.[31]

Thursday, November 21

Afternoon

Although Harvey had been getting rides every Friday to Irving from fellow TSBD employee Buell Wesley Frazier – to visit his wife Marina and his two children on the weekends – he now asked Wesley for a ride to Irving this afternoon. Wesley later told police that Harvey had said he was going to Irving to pick up curtain rods for his room in Dallas. In custody, Harvey denied he said that – as noted above, he was going to see his children.

Ever since Marina and Harvey had come to Dallas, Ruth Paine had hosted Marina in her home, off and on, supposedly in return for Russian lessons from Marina. In all likelihood, however, Ruth was a CIA "babysitter" for Marina and Harvey. During this evening, neither Marina nor Ruth saw Harvey with a rifle, bullets, brown wrapping paper, paper tape or a folded blanket, never saw him make a paper sleeve for a rifle nor saw him go out to Ruth's garage, where Harvey had stored most of his belongings.

Evening

A large party was held at the Dallas mansion of oil baron Clint Murchison. Among the guests were Richard M. Nixon, J. Edgar Hoover, oilman H. L. Hunt and "Mac" Wallace, according to Lyndon B. Johnson's mistress Madeline Brown and Murchison family employee May Newman. Nixon left early, Hoover flew in from Washington D.C. and Lyndon Johnson arrived as the party was beginning to break up, around 11:00. The men, above, then went into a conference room.

Johnson, Hoover, Murchison and Hunt all had problems with the Kennedys. Johnson was going to be dumped as Vice President in 1964, was being investigated for corruption by the Justice Department and was likely to go to prison; JFK was planning to retire Hoover; and the Kennedy administration was going to do away with the oil depletion allowance, depriving the oilmen of many millions of dollars in income.

When Johnson emerged from the meeting, he growled into Madeline Brown's ear, "After tomorrow those goddamn Kennedys will never embarrass me again. That's no threat; that's a promise." He repeated this statement to Brown in a phone call the next morning.[32]

Friday, November 22

12:00 A.M.

Seventeen Secret Service agents assigned to the presidential detail were drinking at the Dallas Press Club, leaving only two firemen to guard the sleeping JFK. Since the Press Club wasn't permitted to serve alcoholic drinks past midnight, sometime after twelve the agents moved on to The Cellar in Fort Worth to continue their imbibing (although The Cellar had no permit to sell alcoholic drinks). Most agents left by 3:00 A.M. – the last one departed at 5:00.[1] No one was later punished or even reprimanded, although agents were forbidden to drink while on presidential assignment.

2:15 A.M.

Head waitress Mary Lawrence, who had known Jack Ruby for the past eight years, was working at the Lucas B & B Restaurant, two doors down from Ruby's other nightclub, the Vegas Club. Lawrence said "Lee Harvey Oswald" entered the restaurant and told her and the night cashier that he was waiting for Jack Ruby. When Ruby came in, the two men sat together, talked for over half an hour and then left.

Lawrence reported this meeting to the Dallas police, and when questioned stuck to her story, insisting that the man with Ruby was "positively Lee Harvey Oswald." And it was. The real one: Lee! Ten days later Lawrence received an anonymous phone call from a man who told her, "If you don't want to die, you better get out of town."[2]

4:30–5:00 A.M.

Bad weather was reported at Red Bird Airport in Dallas, so the abort team co piloted by Plumlee flew to Garland Airport instead, arriving near daybreak. Once the weather had cleared sufficiently, the group left Garland for the ten minute flight to Red Bird. They landed there at about 9:30 or 10:30 A.M.[3]

7:10 A.M.

Harvey had overslept. Marina shook him awake. He got up hurriedly and dressed. He put his wedding band into a small ceramic teacup on Marina's bedside table and placed in its drawer $170 – what was left of his last month's FBI informant's pay of $200. Harvey also had $16 in his pocket at this time. He put his Marine Corp ring on his left ring finger, then an expansion bracelet with the name "Lee" etched on its plate on his left wrist – remember, he expected to die this day.[4]

He was wearing faded light bluish-gray work pants, a white T-shirt with a rounded neck, and an unusual *long-sleeved rust-brown tweed shirt with a pattern*. The shirt had the top three buttons missing, a large hole at the elbow of the right sleeve and was not tucked into his pants. *He did not wear a jacket – never wore a jacket during this day*.[5] It is important to keep these clothes in mind – especially the rust-brown shirt – as the day progresses.

Warren Commission Exhibit 150.

Harvey quickly made a cheese sandwich and grabbed – an apple, put them in a small brown bag, headed out the door and turned left, toward the house where Wesley Frazier lived.

Wesley later said that while looking out the kitchen window of his sister's home he saw Harvey walking toward the house with a long package wrapped in brown paper under an arm. Wesley said the package was about 27" long – or 11" shorter than the paper bag in which the Warren Commission later claimed that Harvey's disassembled rifle supposedly had been wrapped.

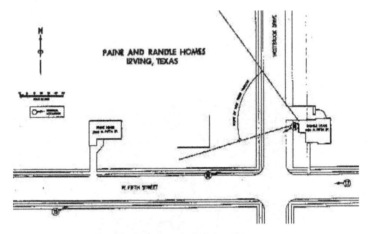

Warren Commission Exhibit 440 –
Paine home left, Randle home right.

Wesley's sister, Linnie Mae Randle, also said she saw Harvey with a 27" package, which he placed on the back seat of Wesley's car. "He opened the right back door, and I just saw that he was laying the package down," she later testified. Only problem with that observation is that it wasn't possible to see what she claimed to see from her kitchen door, where she said she was standing, because a partition in the carport hid Wesley's car from the house, plus it was a cloudy day, right after dawn. And just why did she even look out the kitchen door? For what? Wesley had told her who Harvey was when she saw him through her kitchen window. Actually, he didn't have to tell her. This was the fifth weekend Harvey had driven to Irving with Wesley. Linnie Mae must have seen Harvey earlier.

West side of Randle house, showing the carport and location of Wesley's car as on the morning of November 22.

Wesley's car from the right side, showing the partition..

43

Not only that, but Essie Mae Williams, Linnie Mae's mother, told the FBI that looking through the kitchen window on November 22 she also noticed Harvey coming, and she saw *no* package under either arm.

When Wesley came out of the house, at about 7:20 or 7:25, Harvey was outside the kitchen door. As they got into Wesley's car, Wesley supposedly saw Harvey's package on the back seat, which, he said, Harvey supposedly told him were "curtain rods" that his wife Marina had bought for him for his Dallas "apartment."

It was cloudy, misty as Wesley drove to Dallas. Harvey said little, as usual. They arrived in the parking lot around 7:50. Wesley parked the car and then told Harvey he would charge his car's battery for a few minutes. Harvey exited the car, supposedly got his package, then walked to behind the picket fence and stopped, seemingly waiting for Wesley. However, when Wesley cut the engine off and got out of the car, Harvey started walking away. Wesley followed but didn't catch up with Harvey.[5a]

Wesley later testified that Harvey was carrying his package parallel to his side, with one end stuck in his armpit and the other end held in the palm of his hand. Only problem with that observation is that the distance from Harvey's palm to his armpit was about five inches shorter than the imaginary package, so he could not have been holding it like that. Wesley then saw Harvey enter the TSBD building. Employee Jack Dougherty, who was sitting on the wrapping table near the back door, where Harvey came in, later insisted he didn't see Harvey carry *anything* into the building that morning, nor did anyone else, at any time that day. Harvey went to work as usual, was *assigned* to work on the sixth floor.[6] Coincidence?

The Texas School Book Depository, seen from Houston Street, Dealey Plaza to the left.

Early morning

Before going to work, J. D. Tippit hugged his oldest son Allen and said, "No matter what happens today, I want you to know that I love you." Such signs of open affection toward his son were uncharacteristic of Tippit. This was the

45

last time young Allen saw his father alive.[7]

8:10 A.M.

A TSBD work crew – Charles Givens, Billy Lovelady, Bonnie Ray Williams, Harold Norman and Danny Arce – resumed work laying a new plywood floor on top of the old wood flooring on the sixth floor of the TSBD building. Supervisor Bill Shelley periodically came up during the morning to check how the work was progressing.[8]

10:30 A.M.

Dallas Sheriff Bill Decker held a meeting with all of his available deputies and told them they "were to take no part whatsoever in the security of the presidential motorcade." They were simply to stand in front of the building as the motorcade went by. The assassination took place just down the street.[9]

10:30 – 11:00 A.M.

After the abort team arrived at Redbird Airport, Plumlee was asked if he wanted to be a spotter. He agreed, was added to the part of the team assigned to the south side of Dealey Plaza. Other members of the team were to patrol the north side and the overpass, looking for a triangulation ambush. The group was driven to Dealey Plaza, where from a position on the south knoll Plumlee began to check various areas and attempt to spot potential members of an attack team.[10]

10:50 A.M.

Twenty-three-year-old Julia Ann Mercer was driving west on Elm street, approaching the Triple Underpass. She was halted in heavy traffic, due to a green pickup truck that was illegally parked at the right, two wheels on the curb. As she watched, a white man – in his late twenties or early thirties, wearing a plaid shirt – got out of the passenger seat, removed a rifle case from the back of the truck and climbed up the little hill by the overpass toward the picket fence.

As she slowly pulled even with the truck, she locked eyes with the driver, who sat only a couple of feet from her. Two days later she would recognize him when he shot Harvey Oswald. The man in the driver's seat of the pickup was Jack Ruby.[11]

11:40 A.M.

Air Force One had landed at Love Field. Now the two-pronged process of stripping away security from JFK and preparing for the cover-up slipped into gear.

The bubble top of the presidential limousine was removed. It was not bullet-proof but might have deflected a bullet or reflected the sun and created a problem for

47

shooters. Had it been on, it definitely would have shown the number of shots fired at JFK and the directions they came from. Off came the bubble top.

The motorcycle officers riding by the limousine had been reduced in number to four, and instead of flanking the four corners of the vehicle, they were moved to behind the limousine. Two Secret Service agents – who normally either jogged beside the limousine or stood on platforms at the rear of the vehicle and grasped hand-holds – were waved away by the Special Agent In Charge as the motorcade left Love Field.

When all this was looked into afterwards, the Secret Service claimed that JFK had ordered the bubble top removed, had ordered the motorcycle police to ride behind the car and had ordered the two Secret Service agents not to stand on the back of the limousine. In later years, however, various Secret Service agents said this was not true, that JFK had not ordered these actions, that, in fact, he was very cooperative with the Secret Service and did not interfere with their work. So, some Secret Service personnel were lying.[12]

On the ground in Dallas, policemen who were lining the motorcade route were told to stand facing the street, rather than facing the crowd, as was the norm. Of course, no buildings had been inspected, no windows had been sealed, no sharpshooters were on any roofs, no sheriff's deputies were helping, and there was only light police presence from the corner of Main and Houston Streets on.

Then, preparations for the cover-up. All vehicles in the motorcade had been given numbers at the airport, attached to each vehicle, to indicate its place in the motorcade. Mysteriously, the order of these vehicles got scrambled, as well as the place of some members of the motorcade.

Admiral George Burkley, the President's personal physician, who normally rode in either the lead car or the presidential follow car, was placed – along with Evelyn Lincoln, JFK's secretary – in a bus at the rear of the motorcade. Cecil Stoughton, the White House photographer who normally sat in the Secret Service follow car behind the presidential limousine was replaced by presidential aide Dave Powers.

Next, a flatbed truck for both still and motion picture photographers that had *always* been placed right before the presidential limousine was cancelled at the last minute. No one ever admitted to giving this order or said why it was given. Finally, White House press photographers were placed in a convertible, in the #9 position, other photographers put in three cars behind them, and some journalists were placed 600 feet behind the president's limousine.[13]

Abbreviated list of cars:
    4. Presidential limousine
    5. Secret Service follow-up car
    6. Vice Presidential limousine
    7. Secret Service follow-up car
    9. National Press Pool car
    10. Camera car #1
    11. Camera car #2
    12. Camera car #3
    17. White House Press bus #1
    18. Local Press Pool car
    19. White House Press bus #2
    24. Official Party bus.[14]

Now, it doesn't take a genius to conclude that someone did not want JFK's doctor near him during the motorcade and also wanted news photographers and the press corps as far from the President as possible, so that neither reporters nor cameras would be able to observe or record the assassination. As will be seen shortly, there also were strenuous efforts made to destroy, suppress, ignore and alter most relevant still photos and motion pictures, and similar efforts were employed with witnesses.

No innocent explanation was ever given for the motorcade changes, nor did anyone ever admit to ordering them. All the changes obviously were deliberate, preplanned, designed to help cover up what would occur. And, of course, the route of the motorcade had been changed, so that it would go around the 120° corner of Houston and Elm at only 11 mph.

11:45 A.M.

Foreman Bill Shelley came up to the TSBD sixth floor to lead his crew down for lunch. Seems normal. Except for one thing: the crew usually went down ten minutes later, at 11:55, to start their noon lunch break. One can only speculate that their early departure from the sixth floor was timed to give the assassins an extra ten minutes to prepare.

The men went down in both freight elevators, "racing" each other to the first floor. As they passed the fifth floor, Harvey was there and yelled to them to send one of the elevators back up to him when they got to the first floor.

11:50 A.M.

An elevator apparently *was* sent up because Bill Shelley, on the first floor, saw Harvey standing near a phone at this time. Why was Harvey standing by a phone, instead of going to grab his lunch? Was he waiting for a call or about to make a call? From or to his CIA handler?

12:00 P.M.

The next forty minutes are key to unraveling who fired

from the TSBD, how they got in and got out, who helped them, what was supposed to happen, what did and did not happen and why, what was true and what was false, and who helped to enable and cover up what took place in the TSBD. There were numerous lies, then and later, but many lies were obvious, others inept, so that most – though not all – questions ultimately were answered.

The central player in this tightly-packed mystery within mysteries is not a person, however, but the TSBD building, with its seven floors, three elevators and creaky old stairs. Without examining this brick and mortar enabler – a number of whose inhabitants inadvertently or purposefully became entangled in JFK's murder – major mysteries of November 22 could not have been solved. And take note that of the twenty persons so enmeshed seventeen were employees of just one of the eight companies housed in the structure – the Texas School Book Depository company.

~

Two shooters and their two spotters probably had arrived on the sixth floor by this time, one pair at the farthest southeast "sniper's nest" double windows, the other pair at the farthest southwest double windows.

The question is: how did they get there? No one said they saw them enter the building; no one saw or heard them come up the stairs; no one saw them on the freight elevators; no one saw them anywhere. They could have entered before the building opened in the morning, but then they would have had to wait on the roof or seventh floor and risk being discovered. Most likely, their rifles had been hidden on the sixth or seventh floor the night before, and on this day the four men climbed up the outside fire escape on the east side of the TSBD, three of the men dressed in suits or sport jackets, carrying forged Secret Service documents should they be stopped. They entered from the roof, through a door or hatch, down the stairs to the seventh floor, then to the sixth floor.

DPD patrol sergeant Donald Flusche later said, "[Westphal, Flowers and I] went up into the attic, which was also the seventh floor. There was some thought that the scuttle hole was open up there, and for some reason the manager or somebody in that building thought that was strange…. It also was real strange that with all these federal people standing around…we were the only three that would go up there."[15]

The next question has to be: who unlocked/opened the roof door/hatch for them? And when? The best candidate is Bill Shelley, the man who worked in military intelligence in World War II, the man arrested in 1960 for weapons theft, the man who led his TSBD crew down early, the man who said he stood at the top of the TSBD steps when JFK was shot but didn't, the man who gave different accounts of his actions immediately after the shots, the man who years later told a reporter he had worked for the CIA. That Bill Shelley. He could have gone up and unlocked/opened the roof door/hatch any time during the morning.

~

Meanwhile the employees of the TSBD and of several publishers' reps housed in the TSBD building now started drifting out the front doors to see JFK pass by at 12:25.

Harvey told Black co-worker Eddie Piper, "I'm going up to eat." That means Harvey had retrieved his lunch from somewhere on the first floor and was going to the second floor break room where he often ate and usually bought a Coke, sometimes asking a secretary to make change for the soda machine.

Eddie Piper took his lunch and sat by a first floor front window to eat and watch JFK go by. Troy Eugene West, an older Black worker, who wrapped packages and had been employed by the TSBD for sixteen years, went to make coffee, got his lunch from under the wrapping table (which was situated in the area near the back door), sat on a chair facing the front of the building and started eating.

~

Bonnie Ray Williams, a Black TSBD warehouse worker later testified that he went up to the sixth floor in the east freight elevator at noon to eat his lunch and remained there, eating, sitting between the third and fourth sets of south-facing windows, "from 5, 10, maybe 12 minutes," until "approximately 12:20, maybe," in which span of time he ate a chicken "on the bone" sandwich and a bag of Doritos, drank a bottle of Dr. Pepper. Which sequence is not possible.

First of all, Bill Shelley didn't lead his men downstairs at 11:45 just to have Williams go up there at 12:00. Second, why would Williams go upstairs to eat – and say he expected others to come up there – when almost the entire TSBD work force – including Black employees James "Junior" Jarman and Harold Norman – was outside, waiting for JFK to pass by? Third, street witnesses saw two men in the furthest sixth floor set of southeast windows and two other men in the furthest set of southwest windows, one white man in each set of windows, at 12:15. Williams said he saw no one up there.

And why did Williams decide at 12:20 to go down to the fifth floor? He said he had gone up to the sixth floor to watch the JFK motorcade. Why did he now go looking for others on the fifth floor? Williams came down on the east elevator, near the *northwest* corner of the fifth floor, and Jarman and Norman at that time had just come up on the west elevator and were then at the furthest *southeast* windows. That distance, diagonally, was about 140 feet, and – since the fifth floor also was a storage area for many boxes of books – Williams could not have seen Jarman and Norman (who were kneeling or squatting by their open windows) behind the numerous tall stacks of cartons, and he then couldn't have heard them making any noise, as they were on the other side of the building. In addition, even had Williams' story been true, it would have destroyed the Warren Commission's fairytale that Harvey Oswald had been up on the sixth floor then, preparing to shoot at the President.

Some of Williams' testimony to the WC: [Why did you stop on the fifth floor?] "To see if there was anyone there." [Did you know there was anyone there before you started down?] "Well, I thought I heard somebody walking, the windows moving or something. Maybe someone is down there, I said to myself. And I just went on down." [Did you find anybody there?] "As I remember, when I was walking up, I think Harold Norman and James Jarman – as I remember, they was down facing Elm Street on the fifth floor." [When you got to the fifth floor and left the elevator, at that time were both elevators on the fifth floor?] "Yes, sir." [Both west and east?] "Yes, sir." Here the WC attorney was working to help set up the later false testimonies of Roy Truly and Marion Baker, which will be found below. Jarman testified that he and Norman had come upstairs "about 12:25 or 12:28.... Then we went to the [southeast] front of the building and raised [two] windows. A few minutes later Bonnie Ray Williams [joined us.]" The times obviously don't fit together.

Keep in mind that there was fabrication, alteration and suppression of evidence and testimony, as well as intimidation of and lying by witnesses. Understand also that from this time forward a number of witnesses were murdered. So, as Jim Marrs wrote, not a single piece of evidence or a single sentence of testimony can simply be assumed to be valid. The Williams' transcript appears to contain false testimony.

~

Victoria (Vicki) Adams, Sandra Styles, Elsie Dorman and their supervisor Dorothy Ann Garner, all of whom worked for Scott, Foresman & Co. on the fourth floor, decided to watch the motorcade from the front windows. The four women walked to the third set of windows west of

Houston Street and opened a window to see better.

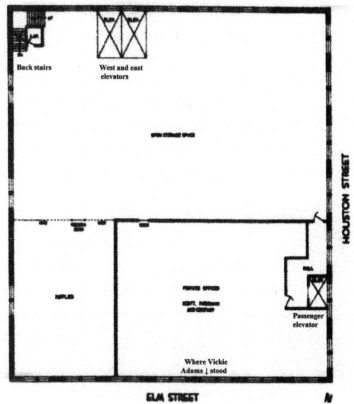

TEXAS SCHOOL BOOK DEPOSITORY
DIAGRAM OF FOURTH FLOOR

Vicki Adams' position.

12:02 P.M.

Ken DuVall, a truck driver with Central Motor Freight, who frequently picked up boxes of books from the TSBD, saw Harvey in the second floor lunchroom about a half hour before the assassination.[16]

12:15 P.M.

Carolyn Arnold, Campbell's secretary, working on the second floor, married and pregnant, prepared to go outside with a coworker to wait for JFK. But first, she craved a glass of water, so she walked over to the lunchroom.

Coke machine is further to the right.

Entering, she saw Oswald. "I do not recall that he was doing anything," she later said. "I just recall that he was sitting there in one of the booth seats on the right hand side of the room as you go in. He was alone as usual and appeared to be having lunch. I did not speak to him, but I recognized him clearly." The time, she said, was "about 12:15. It may have been slightly later."[17] Keep in mind that the motorcade was scheduled to pass by the TSBD building at 12:25.

In addition, there was a 1978 article in *The Dallas Morning News* about Carolyn Arnold, "who states she *definitely* saw Oswald in the *second-floor* lunchroom at *12:25 P.M.*" She told a reporter that the FBI had falsified her statement.[18]

OUTSIDE WITNESSES

Arnold and Barbara Rowland

The young married couple had come to see the President and were standing on the east side of Houston, near the corner of Main, when Arnold happened to look toward the TSBD and saw a young man standing in the southwest-most set of windows of the TSBD's sixth floor. The man was holding a scoped high-powered rifle, had a light-colored shirt, dark pants and dark hair, was proportionately slim with a light complexion. Arnold thought the man was in his early thirties but although Arnold had very good vision, he was a block away from the man, who was three to five feet back inside the building, where "it was more or less not fully light or bright in the room." Arnold also said, "I just didn't get a good look at his face," so the age can only be considered an estimate.

County Inmates

A number of inmates on the sixth floor of the county jail on Houston Street, waiting for JFK to come by, saw two men for several minutes in the TSBD's sixth floor far southwest windows, one man with a rifle that had a scope.

Carolyn Walther

Walther and a co-worker, employees of a dress factory in the Dal-Tex Building, were standing south of the southeast corner of Elm and Houston Streets at about 12:20, when Walther happened to look up at the TSBD building and saw a man standing on either the fourth or fifth floors at the southeast corner windows. He was leaning out an open window, his hands extended outside, holding a rifle with both hands, the barrel pointed downward. The weapon had a short barrel and seemed large around the stock or end of the rifle. The man was wearing a white shirt and had blond or light brown hair, Walther reported.

To his left was another man, standing erect, his head above the open part of the window. Since the window was quite dirty, Walther couldn't see his head – all she saw was his right side, from about the waist to the shoulders, and that he was wearing a brown suit coat. This man would be seen again a couple of minutes after the shooting by two other witnesses.

Amos Lee Euins and L. R. Terry

Euins was a fifteen-year-old high school student, standing on the south side of the Elm and Houston intersection. He not only saw a rifleman in the southeast-most sixth story window but saw him shoot twice. Terry did not see the shooter, just a rifle barrel and a hand in the window.[19]

Richard Randolph Carr

Carr, a steel worker looking for employment, had climbed up to the seventh floor of the new courthouse building that was under construction on Houston and Commerce Streets, facing Dealey Plaza. "I can't recall the exact time, but it was [when] the parade was coming down towards Dealey Plaza..., going to the School Book Depository. Dealey Plaza would have been to my left where I was standing, and at the fifth floor of the School Book Depository I noticed a man at the third window.... I thought he was a Secret [Service] man or an FBI man.... He had on a felt hat, a light hat, he had on heavy-rimmed glasses, dark, and heavy ear pieces on his glasses.... He had on a tie, a light shirt, a tan sport coat."[20]

James "Ike" Altgens

Just before the motorcade came by, Associated Press photographer Altgens later said, a number of people appeared behind the wall on the knoll, to the right of the stairs (facing the knoll), policemen among them. DPD later reported that no policemen had been assigned there.[21]

Lee Bowers

Railroad supervisor Bowers, stationed in a tower about fourteen feet off the ground just north of the "grassy knoll," saw three strange cars, two with out of state license plates, enter the railroad parking lot behind the "grassy knoll" – the first car at 12:10, the second at 12:20, the third a couple of minutes later – and slowly circle around the lot. The driver of the second car appeared to be speaking into a mike or phone. All three seemed to be checking out the area, then drove off. No person exited or entered any one of the cars, and Bowers did not see the cars again.

More to the point, Bowers also saw two strange men in the vicinity of the picket fence, one middle-aged and heavy-set, the other in his mid-twenties and wearing a plaid shirt, which is what James Files said he had on.[22]

Mrs. Louise Velez

Across Houston Street from the TSBD, while waiting for the parade and looking down from the second floor window of a sewing room, Mrs. Velez and two co-workers saw Jack Ruby walking up and down the street by the TSBD.[23] These women probably were employees of McKell's Sportswear, a women's clothing manufacturer in the Dal-Tex Building, 501 Elm Street (below).

Altgens6 detail. Dal-Tex Building, northeast corner of Elm and Houston, across the street from the TSBD entryway. At upper right may have been the women who saw Ruby. They certainly had direct line of sight. Note the man sitting on the fire escape. Why is his jacket on the railing?

Gordon Arnold

Arnold, who recently had completed Army basic training and was dressed in his khakis, came to watch the parade and film it with a movie camera. He parked near Bower's railroad tower and was walking behind the picket fence, when a man in a light suit walked up to him and said Arnold shouldn't be there. When Arnold asked why not, the man showed him a badge and said he was with the Secret Service and didn't want anyone up here. After some more words, Arnold went to the front of the picket fence.

That was the first encounter with a false Secret Service agent in Dealey Plaza, but only the prelude to a traumatic experience Arnold had a few minutes later.

Richard Eaves

Eaves was a college student, married and living in Oak Cliff. He was in Dallas to apply for a part-time job in the advertising department of *The Dallas Morning News*, located at Young and Houston, about four blocks south of Dealey Plaza.

His brother-in-law was DPD Officer W. E. "Gene" Barnett, who was a foot patrolman, stationed at the corner of Commerce and Akard Streets, about a block from Jack Ruby's Carousel Club. Ruby often stopped to chat with Barnett. Eaves mother was the assistant manager at Lucas B & B Restaurant in Oak Lawn for years and knew Jack Ruby. On the night of November 21-22, she saw Ruby talking on the pay phone at B & B at about 2:30 A.M.. He seemed very agitated.

Eaves arrived at the *News* around 12:15 P.M. this day. As he was entering the building, he saw Jack Ruby leaving. Ruby looked preoccupied. Eaves had met Ruby briefly in July or August of 1963, while he was visiting Barnett. As Eaves was speaking with Barnett on the street that day, Ruby came by. He stopped to chat for a moment, and

Barnett introduced Eaves to Ruby, who gave Eaves a business card for the Carousel Club and invited him to come and see one of his "fabulous shows," then walked off.

Now, Eaves went on into the *News* building. When he got to the personnel department, the only one there was the receptionist. She said that everyone else had gone to Dealey Plaza to see JFK.

Bottom line: Ruby was not in the *News* building placing an ad when Kennedy was shot, as he had claimed.[24]

12:20 – 12:25 P.M.

Harvey left the lunchroom, walked through the TSBD secretarial area and down the front staircase. He exited the building, went down the right side of the steps, stopped on the third step from the bottom and leaned his right shoulder against the entranceway's right (facing out) pillar. Bill Shelley was standing to Harvey's left; Billy Lovelady was standing to Shelley's left. Billy was wearing a short-sleeved sport shirt with broad vertical red and white stripes. Harvey was still wearing his rust-brown long-sleeved shirt with the top three buttons missing, leaving the top open. The shirt was hanging out of his trousers, and the front of his white T-shirt was pulled down into a "V," as Harvey had a nervous habit of pulling on the front of his T-shirt.

~

"Junior" Jarman, Harold Norman and Charles Givens had been standing with Daniel Arce, a Mexican, on the sidewalk to the right of the TSBD entranceway. Now, however, Jarman and Norman decided to watch from upstairs. They went around the building on Houston Street, entered through the back door, and got on the west freight elevator, the one with a punch button. Jarman: "[The east] elevator…was up on six, I believe. And we walked around the elevator and took the west elevator up." [How could you tell [the east] elevator was at six?] "Because after we got around to the other side we looked up." [You could see it was on six?] "Yes." [This was about what time?] "That was about 12:25 or 12:28." [You got off on the fifth floor?] "Yes, sir…. We got out the elevator and *pulled the gate down. That was in case somebody wanted to use it.* Then we went to the front of the building, which is on the south side, and raised [two] windows. A few minutes later Bonnie Ray Williams [joined us.]"

12:20- 12:34 P.M.

Geneva Hine was a TSBD secretary with a desk in the large second floor office space. When the other secretaries bemoaned that they would not see the President, Hine volunteered to stay and man the phones. So everyone except Otis Williams went out, and he also left after a few minutes.

Hine went to sit at the middle desk on the front row, on which was a phone with buttons that lit up for calls. When she testified to the WC, she made no mention of any calls coming in at this time: "I was alone until the lights all went out and the phones became dead because the motorcade was coming near us..., so I got up and [went to] the east window in our office.... I saw the escort car come first up the middle of Houston Street, going north.... I saw it turn left and saw the President's car coming and saw the President waving his hand in greeting...and I saw him turn the corner, and just at the instant I saw the next car [the Secret Service car] coming up was when I heard the shots [time: 12:30:47]. I saw people running; I saw people falling down, lying down on the sidewalk.

"My first thought was if I could only see what happened, so I went out our front door into the foyer.... The [passenger] elevator was to my left, and I went past the hall [on] my right and knocked on the door of Lyons and Carnahan.... I tried the door, and it was locked..., and I called, 'Me, please let me in...,' [but] she didn't answer....

"I retraced my steps back to where the hall turned to my left and went down to Southwestern Publishing Co.'s door,

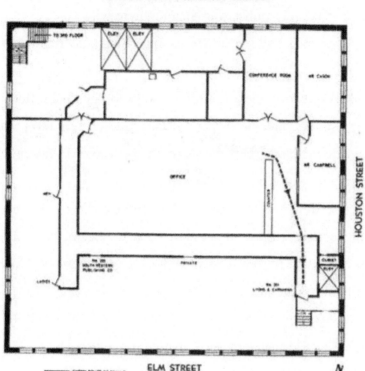

TEXAS SCHOOL BOOK DEPOSITORY
DIAGRAM OF SECOND FLOOR

ELM STREET

and I tried their door...and *there was a girl in there talking on the phone,* and I could hear her but she didn't answer the door.

"I called out to her and shook the door and she didn't answer me because *she was talking on the telephone;* I could hear her. They have a little curtain up, and I could see her form through the curtains. I could see her talking...and

69

then I turned and went through the [west] hall and came through the back door…and I went straight to the desk because the telephones were beginning to wink."

Hine said nothing about seeing TSBD superintendent Roy S. Truly and motorcycle police officer Marion L. Baker or hearing them run up the steps to the second floor. They should have been there at that time [c. 12:32:37], so she should have seen or heard them. The WC attorney didn't question her about the two men.

Asked if she had seen Mrs. Robert Reid: "I don't believe there was a soul in the office when I came back in." Hine said that five or six people then entered together: "Mr. Williams, Mr. Molina, Miss Martha Reid, Mrs. Robert Reid, Mrs. Sarah Stanton, and Mr. O. C. Campbell [c. 12:34]." Told that Mrs. Reid had come in alone [c. 12.33]: "Well, it could be that she did. I was talking on the phones, and then came the policemen and then came the press. Everybody was wanting an outside line." Except that Mrs. Reid never mentioned seeing Hine when Mrs. Reid had entered the office.

Asked about seeing Lee Harvey Oswald enter, Hine said, "My back would have been to the door he was supposed to have come in." She was facing the door by which he was supposed to have left but said she didn't see him leave.

The reason for including this WC testimony – given on April 7, 1964 – is that it is so contradictory, confused and questionable. In summary, Hine testified that 1) the phones were out but that she heard another secretary speaking on a phone; 2) she did not see Mrs. Reid, did not see Oswald, but saw Mrs. Reid with a group (contradicting Mrs. Reid's WC testimony that she returned to the office alone and encountered Oswald); and 3) she didn't see or hear Truly and Baker.

The crucial statement is that the lights went out on the phones, but since she left her desk almost at once, there is nothing to indicate how long those lights were out, as she left the room shortly. Nor is it known if the overhead office lights also went out – or not. What is known, however is that there was no telephone failure anywhere else in Dallas that day.[25]

So the key element, as will be seen, is whether the electricity actually went out, and if it did, when and for how long, since the functioning of the three elevators was in question. All of these issues will subsequently be looked into closely.

12:30 *P.M*

Rose Cherami was still in East Louisiana State Hospital, now watching television in a recreation room. Scenes from Dallas of President Kennedy flashed on the screen. "Somebody's got to do something!" Rose shouted. "They're going to kill the president!" As the motorcade hove into view, Rose cried out, "Watch! This is where it's going to happen! They're going to get him! They're going to get him at the underpass!" No one paid any attention to her.[26]

~

Jack Dougherty was one of only two TSBD employees who made no effort to see JFK, and his later WC testimony was a jumble of contradictions and confusion. He began by stating he got to work at 7:00 A.M., an hour before everyone else, which means he could have opened the door/hatch on the seventh floor for the assassins.

He testified he began eating his lunch at 12:00, resumed work at 12:30 – although lunch break ended at 12:45 – and went up to the sixth floor, at 12:40. [Of course, by then the TSBD was a madhouse – he couldn't have gone up at that time.] He then immediately went down to the fifth floor [!?], using the west elevator, to get some stock, heard one shot and went down to the first floor. So, he is claiming here that he heard a shot at about 12:45.

Asked how he had come downstairs, he said "I used that push button elevator on the west side." [Did you hear Mr. Truly yell anything up the elevator shaft?] "I didn't hear anybody yell." [Did you see any other employee on the fifth floor?] "No, sir; I didn't see nobody –– here wasn't nobody on the fifth floor at all – it was just myself." Of course, Jarman, Norman and Williams were on the fifth floor at that time, and they said the west elevator was not there. And what about the electricity supposedly being out and elevators motionless?

Even a WC lawyer found Dougherty suspicious and asked to have him investigated. All in all, Dougherty's statements are unbelievable and worthless.

~

Outside the TSBD, Superintendent Truly and V. P. Campbell were standing at the curb adjacent to the street signal light to their left. Mrs. Robert A. Reid, a clerical supervisor, stood near Truly; Carolyn Arnold and Virginia Rackley were by Campbell. The people on the landing at the top of the front steps – from east to west – were TSBD employees Pauline Sanders, Joe Molina, Otis Williams, Wesley Frazier and – supposedly – Bill Shelley and Billy Lovelady. Two or three steps down, on the east side, was seventeen-year-old TSBD warehouse worker Roy Edward Lewis; also on that step were MacMillan Publishing employees Ruth Dean and Madie Reese, to Lewis' left. On the third step from the bottom – from west to east – were – seemingly – four men (who will be discussed shortly), with Scott, Foresman employees Avery Davis and Judy McCully to their left. TSBD employee Sarah Stanton was one step below the man farthest east, who was standing behind her.[27]

The locations and identities of these individuals, seemingly unimportant, are actually crucial to determine where Harvey Oswald was when the fatal shots were fired. Anchoring the entire issue is one photograph, Altgens6 (below), taken by James Altgens a moment after JFK was struck in the throat. The TSBD entranceway looms in the background.

It has been well-established over the years that assassination still photographs and motion pictures were ignored, made to vanish, destroyed and tampered with while in the custody of the FBI. Although the Bureau had considerable success in this effort, it was unable to accomplish all of its goals, due in part to computers and other technology that came into existence later. Nor did the Bureau expect the intense scrutiny of the assassination evidence, testimony and lies by thousands of citizen investigators over the next six decades.

The first thing to strike a viewer of the Altgens6 photo is the Stygian blackness in the upper half of the TSBD

Altgens6, by James Altgens, taken just after the first shot hit JFK.

entranceway (above): no light reflected from a face, an eye, a hand, from glass, from metal – nothing, not the slightest glimmer of the people said to be standing up there. That is especially noticeable, since this was a bright, sunny day.

Further, other photographs taken shortly after Altgens6 – such as the ones below – reveal people and the glass and metal entrance at the top of the stairs, as well as the ceiling and a metal hand rail running down the middle of the steps. There is no way to get around the blackness in Altgens6 being superimposed on all those behind and above the individuals seen standing near the bottom of the entrance-

Detail of Altgens6. The sun was shining directly into the entranceway at this moment. Arrow was drawn by Wesley Frazier during WC testimony.

About 1:00 to 1:15 P.M. Note that the men on upper steps – one on the landing exactly where Wesley Frazier had said he'd stood – are easily seen.

way. That part of Altgens6 obviously was painted black to hide something or someone. But who, or what? The answer to that question was many years coming but it finally

arrived: the blackness didn't hide what was under it – it hid what *wasn't* under it. Because although Bill Shelley and Billy Lovelady claimed they were on the top landing when Altgens6 was created, they actually were standing on the third step up from the bottom.

How is this known? Because all other TSBD male employees stated they stood elsewhere, as did all the male employees of the other companies in the TSBD building. Then who was at the bottom of the steps? Let's look at a blowup of a detail of Altgens6 to discover what was done to the picture and why.

In the image is seen as bizarre a sight as you'll ever behold in a supposedly real photo. Sticking out of the pillar on the left is the profile of a Black man. In back of this face is a man with no left shoulder, beside who is a man simultaneously behind and before him, missing the top half of his head. To his left is a headless man shading his

Detail from Altgens6.

missing eyes with his hands. Below and between these two men is some extra hair attached to a Black woman's head, above which is what looks like an artificially created reclining man. If you study the white blobs above the woman's left, you realize those areas have been whited out with some liquid – see the jagged, unformed left shirt edge of the man at the right of the photo and the right arm of the man in front of him. Finally, the man with the tie, facing right, is something arbitrary that was inserted to hide Bill

Shelley, as there was no such man known to have been standing on the stairs.

The reason for these crude alterations is simple. Harvey Oswald was the man by the pillar and, next to him, made to disappear, was Bill Shelley, beside who was Billy Lovelady in a short-sleeved shirt. Harvey had Lovelady's forehead (taken from the "headless man") superimposed on him, to make him appear to be Lovelady. So all of this manipulation was designed with one aim in mind: show that the figure was not Harvey Oswald but Billy Lovelady. Below are the faces of Billy, "Altegens6 man" (extraneous

| Billy | Altgens6 | Harvey |

material removed from his left) and Harvey: Altgens6 clearly is not Billy, can only be Harvey.

To show how ridiculous the FBI and Warren Commission were, below are the shirts worn by all three. Note that Billy has a short-sleeved shirt, just like the man in Altgens6. Not only was the Altgens6 shirt identical in color, cut, pattern and texture to Harvey's , but both shirts had the top three buttons missing and the apparent V-neck of the Altgens6 T-shirt, due to Harvey's nervous habit of

Billy   Altgens6   Harvey

tugging at his T-shirt. The posture and facial expression in Altgens6 also were typical of Harvey.

So where did Shelley and Lovelady say they stood? Bill Shelley, to the Warren Commission: "I went outside then, to the front.... Several people were out there..., Lloyd Viles and Sarah Stanton.... Wesley Frazier and Billy Lovelady joined us shortly afterwards." [Standing where?] "Just outside the glass doors." [That would be on the top landing of the entrance?] "Yes." However Pauline Sanders, Joe Molina and Otis Williams said they were on the landing at 12:30, and then Shelley said (below) that Carolyn Arnold also was up there. That would make nine people on the landing. There wasn't enough room up there for all those people.

In another statement Shelley said, "Lovelady was seated on the entrance steps in front of me.... Wesley

Frazier, Mrs. Sarah Stanton and Mrs. Carolyn Arnold were also standing near me.... I did not see Lee Harvey Oswald." However, Arnold stated she was standing with Campbell, Viles said he was on the south side of Elm Street. Only Shelley put Frazier on the landing – no one else even mentioned seeing him.

Then Billy Lovelady, to the Warren Commission: [You ate your lunch on the steps?] "Yes, sir." [Who was with you?] "Bill Shelley and Sarah Stanton." [Where were you when the picture was taken? (Shown Altgens6)] "Right there at the entrance of the building standing on the step, would be here." [You were standing on which step?] *"It would be your top level."* [The top step, you were standing there?] "Right."*

However, a May 24, 1964 *New York Herald-Tribune* article, reported by Dom Bonafederted, stated, *"'I was standing on the first step,'* [Lovelady] told me when I interviewed him.... 'Several people saw me. That lady shielding her eyes [Sarah Stanton, standing below the headless figure] works here on the second floor.'" Then Billy must have been the headless figure standing right behind her. He ate his lunch at the top of the steps after he came out and then went down with Shelley to the third step. So, Billy apparently told the truth when he said he was with

Shelley and Stanton – he only lied, at first, about what step he stood on at 12:30.

It needs also to be noted that Billy pointed to the figure leaning against the pillar in Altgens6 as being his picture – which figure clearly is neither at the top of the steps nor sitting, nor wearing a striped shirt. Two other witnesses also revealed his lies. Ruth Dean, who worked for the MacMillan Publishing Co. told a researcher, "I was standing there with Madie Reese and Billy Lovelady and several other employees. I remember Billy being there because we were joking."[28] Recall that Roy Edward Lewis was standing on about the fifth step up next to those two women. Altgens6 shows neither Lewis nor the two women next to the figure against the pillar. However, Dean very well could have been joking with the headless figure (Billy), while standing behind and to Billy's left. And Lewis added, "I've been told that some people confused Billy Lovelady with Oswald, but Lovelady was much heavier."[29]

Joe Molina: "At approximately 12:20 P.M....I left my office and took a position on the top step of the entrance of the Texas School Book Depository. Otis Williams...and Mrs. Pauline Sanders were also viewing the motorcade with me." No mention of Shelley, Lovelady, Frazier, Viles,

Arnold or Stanton.

What did Wesley Frazier say? He told the WC: "I was standing on the steps...pretty close to Mr. Shelley and this boy Billy Lovelady...[and a] lady...whose name is Sarah [Stanton].... I was...one step down from the top there...standing there by the rail.... [At the sound of the shots – ?] "I stood right where I was." [And Mr. Shelley was still standing there?] "Right." [And also Billy Lovelady?] "Yes, sir...." The same Sarah Stanton that Billy said was at the *bottom* of the steps, and the same Billy who said he was on the bottom step.

However, at the New Orleans Clay Shaw trial in 1969 – now no FBI agents or Dallas police detectives threatening him – Wesley finally told the truth: "When I was standing there at the top of the stairs I was...by a heavyset lady...her name is Sarah [Stanton]." [Anyone else...?] "*Right down in front of me at the **bottom** of the steps my foreman Bill Shelley and Billy Lovelady were standing there.*" But Wesley still feared for his life to venture that Harvey also was standing down there. And since both Billy and Wesley claimed Sarah Stanton, it very well may be that Wesley also was near the bottom of the steps. In any case, Billy was not the figure leaning against the pillar.

So Harvey was leaning against the pillar, Bill Shelley to

his left (just as he would tell Homicide Captain Will Fritz later in the day) and Billy Lovelady to Shelley's left – proving that Harvey did not shoot President Kennedy, in spite of the doctored Altgens6 photo. The reason for the blackness at the top of the entranceway in Altgens6 is now clear.

POSITION OF SHOOTERS

The shooters were spread out in a northern semicircle around Dealey Plaza, from the south knoll to the Records Building:

1. The south knoll. This was the only place Frank Sturgis, CIA-run Operation 40 member, could have been shooting from with his scoped and silenced rifle, accompanied by a spotter, an anti-Castro Cuban exile member of Operation 40.

Tosh Plumlee later wrote he thought he heard four or five shots, one from behind and to his left on the south knoll, near the underpass and south parking lot. He walked over to that area after the shots and smelled gunpowder. Marita Lorenz later said that Sturgis had told her she had missed "the really big one" in Dallas. "We killed the president that day."[30]

A woman being videotaped by a TV journalist was overheard saying that she saw a shot being fired from the south side of the railroad overpass, and there is said to be photographic evidence of what appears to be a person holding a rifle standing in the area on the south knoll that Plumlee walked through shortly afterward.[31]

2. West stockade fence. Behind this structure, recruited by David Atlee Phillips, was James Files, wielding a single-shot Remington Fireball XP-100 (below), given to him by Phillips and loaded with a mercury-filled bullet.[32]

3. Fifteen feet north of the corner of the stockade fence. "Badge man," Lucien Sarti, Corsican assassin, recruited by the CIA through the American Mafia, holding a scoped and silenced rifle, assisted by a 'railroad employee' to take away Sarti's rifle.

4. Southwest-most pair of sixth floor TSBD windows. Operation 40 member Lee Oswald, holding a high-powered rifle with a scope but no silencer, with a spotter, an anti-Castro Cuban exile member of Operation 40.

5. Sixth floor southeast-most pair of TSBD windows,

the "sniper's nest." "Mac" Wallace, with a rifle that had no silencer and an Operation 40 dark-skinned anti-Castro Cuban exile assisting him.

6. Dal-Tex Building, second floor, second window north. The second Corsican Mafia assassin, the "low" – almost horizontal – shooter, with a scoped and silenced rifle. Possible spotter sitting on the fire escape steps.

7. Records Building, roof. Third Corsican assassin, the "high" shooter, with a scoped and silenced rifle and a likely spotter. Witness Elsie Dorman felt shots were coming from the Records Building.[33]

There also may have been a shooter in a storm drain to the right of the limousine, which will be discussed further on in this narrative.

Deputy Sheriff Harry Weatherford was ordered with his rifle to the top of the County Jail building by Sheriff Bill Decker. Weatherford was said to have received a custom-made silencer for his rifle several weeks before the assassination.[34]

12:30:47 – 12:30:53

THE HIT

As the presidential limousine drew even with the Stemmons Freeway sign on Elm Street, JFK was hit by a bullet in his throat, just above the knot in his tie. His forearms and elbows flew up near his chin, his hands looking almost as if he were clutching his throat. For the next six seconds, bullets rained down on the limousine, and JFK began to lean toward his left. Texas Governor John Connally, on a jump seat beside his wife and in front of JFK, was then struck by a bullet, possibly two, from the rear, and fell toward his left.

JFK next was struck by two shots from the third volley, one from the south knoll hitting near his left temple and blowing a large hole in the back of his head on the lower right side, the other shot, from the rear, entering his skull in the area of the large hole. A split second later, a frangible bullet coming from behind the west stockade fence hit him in his right temple from the front, exploding into many tiny pieces inside his skull. He was propelled violently backward and to his left, falling into his wife's lap.

COMPLICITY

The presidential limousine had slowed to 11 mph to navigate the 120° Elm/Houston corner, but rather then speeding up as required by Secret Service regulations, Secret Service driver Bill Greer *slowed down* the vehicle to about 5 mph, then steered the car toward the left curb and, as the first shots rang out, *stopped* the limousine – brake lights showing – instead of stepping on the gas and taking evasive action. Now we know why driver Tom Shipman was murdered in October.

Eyewitness Bill Newman: "I can remember seeing the tail lights of the car, and just for a moment they hesitated and stopped."[35]

"In the Orville Nix film, the brake lights can be seen coming on after the first shot."[36]

Vince Palamara has written that he has documented seventy witnesses who said the limousine slowed or stopped.[37]

That was not all Greer did. He turned around after the first shot and looked at JFK. When Greer's supervisor, agent Roy Kellerman, sitting beside him, ordered Greer to, "Get out of line, we've been hit," Greer ignored the order and turned to stare at JFK for a second time, until JFK was struck with the fatal head shot. Then Greer stepped on the gas.[38]

"UMBRELLA MAN" AND "RADIO MAN"

With so many shooters, coordination was required. Two strange men have been put forward as probable communicators for the gunmen: an umbrella-wielding man and a dark-skinned man with a walkie-talkie.

Umbrella Man came to Dealey Plaza with a long black umbrella, although the day had been clear and sunny since 9:30 A.M. and no one else had an umbrella. He stood on the north side of Elm Street near the Stemmons Freeway sign and kept his umbrella closed until the exact moment that JFK's limousine passed him, whereupon he opened and repeatedly pumped the umbrella up into the air about twenty-four inches, twirled it, then brought it back down.

Radio Man, standing near Umbrella Man, shot his right fist up into the air when the firing began. As soon as the fatal shot hit JFK and the limousine accelerated, Umbrella Man closed his umbrella.

In addition to signaling the shooters, Umbrella Man may also have been signaling driver Bill Greer where to stop the limousine for the final fusillade.

Neither Umbrella Man nor Radio Man looked concerned that JFK's head was blown apart. Showing almost professional detachment, the two seeming strangers now sat down close together on the grass by the curb, their feet on the roadway. Radio Man was photographed with his right hand holding some object to his face, apparently speaking into it, an antenna sticking out behind his head.[39] Soon afterward, the men got up, Umbrella Man walking

Radio Man and Umbrella Man.

east, Radio Man walking west, as he shoved his walkie-talkie into his left rear pants pocket.

So the question is, why do two seeming strangers standing near each other – and acting very oddly – then calmly sit down beside each other on the curb after JFK is shot, while everyone else is running or dropping to the grass in terror, unless they were part of the ambush?

SECRET SERVICE

About five feet behind the presidential limousine when the shots rained down was the Secret Service follow car, a convertible with running boards, on which stood four agents. Four more agents were seated in the car, along with presidential aides Dave Powers and Kenny O'Donnell. Agent Clint Hill, Jacqueline Kennedy's personal agent, stood on the front position of the left running board. Agent Jack Ready stood on the front position of the right running board. Agent in Charge Emory P. Roberts sat beside the driver.

At the sound of the first shot and seeing something wrong with JFK, Clint Hill immediately jumped off the follow car and ran toward the presidential limousine, reaching for a handhold. Agent Ready also jumped off the car but was called back by Roberts, who then told all of his agents not to move.

So not only were there no agents standing on the back of the presidential limousine and no motorcycle police at JFK's side, but Secret Service agents in the follow car were ordered to take no action, even when only five feet separated the two vehicles. Nothing normal about any of this – highly irregular. In addition, some Zapruder film frames were removed of the seconds before, during and after the shooting, which may have depicted actions of Secret Service agents and Dallas police officers of which we are unaware even now.

Agent Hill was able to scramble onto the trunk of the limousine just as Mrs. Kennedy was crawling onto the trunk, apparently trying to retrieve a piece of her husband's skull. Hill pushed her back onto the rear seat, then placed his body on top of hers and the President's – seconds too late to save the President.

NUMBER AND PLACEMENT OF SHOTS

Shots came from both the front and the rear. Neither of the two rifles firing from the TSBD seem to have had silencers, nor did James Files' pistol. Two or three non-silenced shots must have been fired from the TSBD, plus the final shot by James Files. So there were four shots whose muzzle blasts were heard by witnesses. Those who said they heard more shots were hearing bullets breaking the sound barrier, not muzzle blasts.

Some people spoke of a "flurry" of shots or a "volley" of shots, including Secret Service agent Roy Kellerman. Considering the number of bullets that appear to have been fired, it seems likely that – corresponding to the three shots heard by many – three volleys were fired. Files seems to have fired a split second after the third volley.

Witness A. J. Millican, who was standing on the north side of Elm Street, a few feet east of the Stemmons sign, reported in a signed statement: "Just after the President's car passed, I heard three shots come from up toward Houston and Elm, right by the Book Depository Building, and then I immediately heard two more shots come from *the arcade between the [Depository] and the underpass*, and then three more shots came from the same direction only sounded further back...."

Millican's account certainly suggests three volleys. It also suggests there were shooters behind the arcade.[41] Witness Steven F. Wilson stated, "It seemed like the shots came from the west end of the building or the colonnade [arcade]."[42]

As far as the order of shots, if there actually were three volleys, and only three or four shots were heard by most, there is no way to determine the exact order of shots, except that the first shot to hit JFK was in his throat and the last two hit him in his head. A bullet that bounced off the roadway may have been the first shot, meant to misdirect witnesses.

The other thing that's certain is that a separate bullet hit Governor John Connally after a bullet hit J FK and before the fatal shot:

"Nellie Connally, sitting next to her husband in the presidential limousine, always maintained that two bullets struck John Kennedy, and another one hit her husband. [Mrs. Connally:] 'The first sound, the first shot, I heard, and turned and looked right into the President's face. He was clutching his throat, and just slumped down. He just had a – a look of nothingness on his face. He – he didn't say anything. But that was the first shot. The second shot, [which] hit John – well, of course, I could see him covered with – with blood, and his – his reaction to a second shot. The third shot, even though I didn't see the President, I felt the matter all over me, and I could see it all over the car.'"[43]

The reported shots:

1. Two shots that hit the roadway.

Witness Arthur Miller: "One shot apparently hit the street past the car."

Witness Royce Skelton: "I saw something hit the pavement at the left rear of the car...then heard two more shots...then heard another shot and saw the bullet hit the pavement. The concrete was knocked to the south away from the car. [The bullet] hit the left or middle lane."[44]

Ricky Chism, son of witnesses Mr. and Mrs. John Chism, has stated that his parents said the first shot hit the ground – they could see a spark hit the ground.[45]

2. A bullet mark on the south curb of Elm Street. The City of Dallas removed that section of curb.

Stavis Ellis, a motorcycle policeman: "The first shot went off…. I could see where [it] came down into the south side of the curb. It looked like it hit the concrete or grass there…and a bunch of junk flew up…like smoke coming out of the concrete;"[46]

3. A bullet which hit JFK's neck just above the knot

Altgens7. Bullet hole in windshield (in circle).

of his tie, coming through the windshield – left of center (right of the driver) – of the Presidential limousine[47] (seen in the Altgens7 photograph, above), shot from the south knoll, probably by Frank Sturgis.

Numerous people reported seeing a hole in the windshield, including two motorcycle policemen and a Secret Service agent. The hole was big enough to push a pencil through. A glass manager at the Ford Motor Company's Rouge Plant, George Whitaker, reported that the inside chipping showed a frontal entry. Glass shards [were] embedded in JFK's face.[48]

Dr Evalea Glanges, a first year medical student at Parkland Hospital stated, "It was very clear; it was a through and through bullet hole, through the windshield of the car…. It seemed like a high velocity bullet that had penetrated from front to back."[49]

4. A bullet strike to the right of JFK's left temple, coming from the south knoll. The reason this shot did not come through the windshield is that Elm Street is on an incline down toward the underpass, so the shooter – at the same elevation as the overpass – now could look down over the top of the windshield and have a clear shot at JFK's head. This shot, part of the last volley before the kill shot, probably caused the large hole in the back of JFK's head, since the kill shot exploded into tiny pieces inside JFK's head, rather than exiting, creating the blood halo seen on the Zapruder film. Keep in mind, too, that JFK was seated

flush with the right side of the limousine, waving to people, and that the car was angled 120° to the left. The fact that no additional motion of JFK's body was seen from this shot may be due to the rear shot hitting at the same time as this frontal shot or that the motion of JFK's body was edited out of the Zapruder film.

5. A shot in the back of JFK's head, part of the final volley, entrance and exit wounds not seen.

"Evidence shows a second shot struck the president's head from behind: …two killing shots to the head from opposite directions in the final second of the shooting;"[50]

6. A shot, a split second later, in JFK's head from the west picket fence, an explosive bullet, the kill shot.

7. A through and through wound to Governor Connally's back, also through Connally's right wrist (two grams of bullet fragments, the weight of about 1.5 bullets, left in his wrist), three bullet fragments in his left thigh.

8. A bullet that hit the south curb of Main Street near the Triple Underpass and wounded spectator James Tague.

9. A furrow in the grass near a manhole cover on the south curb of Elm Street; a man was photographed picking up something in the grass there and putting it in his pocket.

10. Two grooves pointing southeast in the grass, made by bullets, on the south side of Elm Street, seen by Edna

and Wayne Hartman and a policeman – the policeman and other bystanders pointing to the "grassy knoll."

11. A bullet through the Stemmons Freeway sign, which sign the City of Dallas removed later that day.

12. An indentation in the chrome frame of the Presidential limousine's windshield, to the left of the right visor.

13. A dent on the back of the rearview mirror of the limousine (meaning the bullet came from the front).

14. A bullet hole in the leather at the top of the back of JFK's seat, to his right, bullet from the front.

15. C. E. Johnson, railroad worker, who stood on top of the overpass when JFK was shot: "Later, they were digging around down there where a woman and a little child were sitting. I think the woman said, 'It's a wonder we didn't get shot because the bullet went in right there.' They kept digging and finally found the bullet. I never saw the bullet dug out of the ground, but I heard a lot of people talking about it."[51]

16. Dallas Parkland Hospital nurse Phyllis Hall: "I could see a bullet lodged between [JFK's] ear and his shoulder [under the skin]. It was pointed at its tip and showed no signs of damage…. It was about one-and-a-half inches long – nothing like the bullets that were later

produced.... A doctor removed it, falling on the table.... It was taken away." [She] said it was one of the least damaged bullets she had ever seen. She also stated that the bullet never turned up in the Warren Report. This bullet may have been undercharged (accounting for its almost pristine condition – may have been intended to just shock JFK and immobilize him). Considering its virtually undamaged condition, this may have been "the magic bullet" of Warren Commission fame.[52]

17. An FBI report by Alan Belmont dated 11/22/63 to Clyde Tolson noted that a bullet "was lodged behind the President's ear."[53]

There also were reports of a wound in JFK's chest, and a number of bullet fragments were found in the limousine.

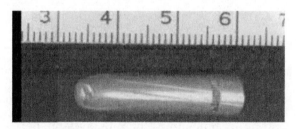

Commission Exhibit 399: Supposedly the bullet found on a stretcher at Parkland Hospital.

Vince Palamara in *Honest Answers* reported the following bullets:

Lt. Day...estimated the distance from the sixth floor window...to where one of the bullets was recovered at one hundred yards.[54]

Richard Dudman reported: "A police inspector told me they had just found another bullet in the grass."[55]

A photo was printed in the *Fort Worth Star-Telegraph* of a rifle bullet lying "in the grass across from Elm Street."[56]

Of course, these three reports could have been of the same bullet.

James Files said he fired the kill shot. He had aimed for Kennedy's right eye but another shot, from the rear, a split second before Files' shot, struck the back of Kennedy's head, moving it forward just as Files fired – hitting Kennedy in his right temple.[57]

Carolyn Walther told investigator Barry Ernest that Abraham Zapruder, whom she knew, told her at the scene, "They got him in the forehead, from the front."[58]

Carl Renas of the Ford Motor Company, driving the presidential limousine from Washington D.C. to Cincinnati, saw several bullet holes in it, the most notable being on the windshield chrome molding strip, which he said clearly was "a primary strike" and not from a bullet fragment.[59]

Walther, also a witness in Dealey Plaza, said she heard four shots, as did another witness, S. M. Holland, who said the third and fourth shots came at "almost exactly the same second," while Walther said those shots seemed to be fired "at the same time." Holland also told Barry Ernest that the kill shot from the grassy knoll sounded "different...like it was a pistol...," corroborating the weapon James Files used. A third witness, Emmett Hudson, a groundskeeper standing on the steps going up the "grassy knoll," said the kill shot, fired to Hudson's right, "...was a bit unusual... louder, sharper, cleaner...and two of them was close together." Holland and Hudson said the kill shot came from the grassy knoll, "the far corner of the wooden fence on top of the knoll," Files' location.[60]

Almost universally, witnesses said that the first shot they heard sounded like "a firecracker." It now seems that it really was a diversionary firecracker. And fifty-one witnesses said that rifle fire came from the front, from the "grassy knoll."

In order to tie the 'three shots' fired at JFK to the Italian 6.5mm Carcano carbine *supposedly* owned by Harvey, some of the bullets had previously been fired into water from the Carcano, retrieved, put into sabots, then fired at JFK – to frame Harvey.

A sabot is a plastic jacket which is placed around a bullet that's smaller than its casing. The sabot protects the

A bullet with a plastic sabot around it in its casing.

bullet's original rifling marks, so that investigators recovering the bullet will think it came from the original weapon, complete with the original rifling marks – in this case, from the Carcano. A sabot reportedly was found on the ground in Dealey Plaza on the afternoon of November 22 by a civilian, and in 1975 a 30.06 shell casing with a crimp around its edge, indicating that a sabot had been used, was found on the roof of the Records Building.[61]

Ed Hoffman

The most striking account of what took place behind the wooden picket fence came from twenty-six year old deaf mute Virgil Edward Hoffman. He was standing about two hundred yards west of the railroad parking lot, where Stemmons Freeway crosses Elm Street, at an elevation of about the first floor of the TSBD, looking down at the area in back of the picket fence.

Hoffman saw two men behind the fence, one a stocky man in a dark blue business suit and black hat, the other a tall man dressed as a railroad worker. The "railroad man" stood next to a switch box by railroad tracks, while the "suit man" repeatedly walked back and forth from the picket fence to the "railroad man." Hoffman also noticed a light green Rambler station wagon come into the parking lot, stopping near a railroad switching tower.

The "suit man" returned a final time to the picket fence and picked up something from the ground. Hoffman saw a puff of smoke by the "suit man," who then turned with a rifle in his hands and ran over and tossed the rifle to the "railroad man," who caught it and with a twist broke it into two parts, thrust it into a railroad worker's soft brown tool bag and then strolled nonchalantly north along railroad tracks.

The "suit man" then turned and began walking casually behind the picket fence, as a police officer came rushing around the fence, pistol drawn. The "suit man" showed his empty hands, then took from a pocket what seemed to be identification [probably one of Chauncey Holt's forged Secret Service IDs] and showed it to the policeman, who then holstered his gun.

The "suit man" melted into the crowd of people who now were flooding the area, then walked over to the Rambler station wagon and got in on the passenger side. The wagon drove out of the lot along the north side of the

103

TSBD and turned right on Houston Street. The vehicle was soon seen elsewhere, with other passengers, which will be recounted shortly.[62]

Deputy Constable Seymour Weitzman also encountered a bogus 'Secret Service agent,' who was on the "grassy knoll" ordering people out of the area. Weitzman later identified the man as Bernard Barker, who was one of the Watergate burglars and was once affiliated with the Miami Mob and the CIA.[63]

Although Hoffman tried to communicate what he had seen, he was warned by his father and uncle not to do so. When he finally went to the FBI, an agent told him, "You'd better keep quiet. You could get killed." It was 1989 before Hoffman's story got out, in Jim Marr's book *Crossfire*.

PHOTOS AND PHOTOGRAPHERS

There were numerous individuals with still cameras and movie cameras taking photographs near the presidential limousine at the time of the assassination. The following four photographers stand out, both because of what they photographed and because of the way their film, and sometimes the photographer, were treated after the shots.

Keep in mind that there were *no* police officers posted by the DPD behind the picket fence or on the "grassy knoll," nor were there any Secret Service agents deployed anywhere in Dealey Plaza, according to the DPD and the Secret Service. There are indications that one or two individuals in a building east of the kill zone were observing the area with binoculars and were identifying and targeting those with cameras along Elm Street west of Hudson. Who were these men?

Abraham Zapruder

The 26 second Zapruder home movie film became famous not simply for its images of the assassination but also for the many years of analysis by researchers, which revealed frames were switched, frames were removed and images were altered by some private or government entity.

Zapruder, a clothing manufacturer, had been filming the motorcade while standing on a four foot high concrete abutment on the north side of Elm Street, not far from the Stemmons Freeway sign (see photo below), braced by his receptionist, Marilyn Sitzman. Zapruder never reported being harassed by anyone afterwards, but he did state that shots came from behind him (from the picket fence) and that JFK had been hit in the right temple from the front.

James "Ike" Altgens

It has already been shown that the Altgens6 photo was manipulated to help make Harvey the assassination's patsy.

What is astonishing is how quickly the photo was targeted and altered, because that seems to have taken place within the first two hours after Altgens turned in his photos.

Mary Moorman and Jean Hill

The second most famous assassination still photo after Altgens6 – not only for what it contains but also for how the two women and the photographs they took were treated – is the Moorman Polaroid. Hill and Moorman were standing near the south curb of Elm Street about half way between Houston Street and the Triple Underpass when the motorcade turned onto Elm.

Jean Hill, Mary Moorman

Moorman began snapping Polaroid pictures, while Hill applied fixative to each photo. As the presidential limousine approached them, Hill yelled, "Hey, Mr. President, look this way. We want to take your picture." As JFK began turning toward the two women, he was hit, then his head exploded. The Moorman photo was snapped just as the fatal shot struck the President.

Hill told Jim Marrs, "I saw a man fire from behind the wooden fence. I saw some sort of movement on the "grassy knoll" where he was [about fifteen feet north of the corner of the picket fence]." Hill heard between four and six shots. Then she noticed a man walking west rapidly in front of the Texas School Book Depository, who she later discovered was Jack Ruby.[64]

Moorman had dropped to the ground when the firing began, but Hill ran across the street and up the "grassy knoll." She rushed behind the picket fence, but all she saw were railroad workers and policemen, some of whom, of course, may have been neither.

When she then began walking toward the TSBD she was accosted by two men who identified themselves as Secret Service agents and who insisted she had to go with them. They hustled her into a building east of the plaza and took her upstairs, where a couple of other men told her *they* were Secret Service agents. One man said he had been watching her and Moorman from a window. She eventually was reunited with Moorman, who had also been brought into this building.

The women's six photographs wound up in the hands of

federal authorities. Three of the photos were returned that day, the other three only weeks later. The backgrounds of two of those pictures were now mutilated, and there was a

Moorman "grassy knoll" photograph.

The "grassy knoll," arrows showing the positions of Badge Man: and Zapruder.

large fingerprint on the lower right corner of the third, the "grassy knoll" picture (below), defacing that area of the photo.[65]

Four months later Hill had an extraordinary encounter with WC counsel Arlen Specter, during which he tried to coerce her to change her account. Afterwards, she stated that her testimony as presented by the WC did not accurately reflect what she'd said.[66] She also was hounded for years by FBI agents, and she characterized the WC Report as a fraud and a hoax.[67]

During subsequent years, researchers pored over the "grassy knoll" photograph, looking for any indication of an assassin. Finally, after two decades, Gary Mack and Jack White were able to bring forward the image, below, of

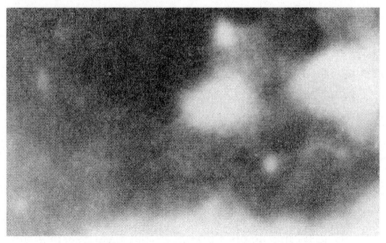

*Badge Man, showing head, muzzle blast hiding
lower part of face, with 'badge' below the blast.*

Badge Man." They took the photo to the Massachusetts Institute of Technology, where they were told that, without question, the photo showed a man firing a rifle.[68]

Gordon Arnold

Arnold had begun filming the motorcade from his spot on the "grassy knoll" three feet before the picket fence "*just after the [limousine] turned onto Elm,*" he later said, when a shot went off behind him. During his Army basic training, Arnold had been required to crawl on the ground while live machine gun fire passed above him, so he had the experience of bullets flying by. Arnold "felt" the bullet go by his left ear, "rather than heard it," then heard a "crack" (not a "bang"). Arnold hit the dirt, and a second shot passed over his head. U.S. Senator Ralph Yarborough, two cars behind the presidential limousine, saw Gordon drop to the ground when the shots rang out. Arnold, still flat on the ground, then "heard several other shots."

The Zapruder film indicates that JFK was shot in the throat while behind the Stemmons Freeway sign, and spectator Phillip Willis later said, "I got the nearest, best [photo] while JFK was behind the [Stemmons] sign. He was upright and waving to the crowd. A split second later, he was grabbing at his throat."[69] That clearly establishes that the first bullet to hit JFK was the one to his throat. No "magic bullet" striking JFK and Connally from the rear, as the WC claimed.

As for "Badge Man," there is no way he could have fired through the windshield and hit JFK's throat – the limousine was angled away from "Badge Man," who was located behind both Arnold and Zapruder, to the left of Arnold and to the right of Zapruder. So the view that the Zapruder film shows (below) must have been almost the same as what the shooter saw before the presidential limousine passed behind the Stemmons sign.

Zapruder film, just before the Stemmons sign (right).

If Frank Sturgis was indeed on the south knoll and fired the shots which struck JFK in the throat and left temple, and James Files fired the kill shot to JFK's right temple, it would mean that "Badge Man" missed JFK with both shots that flew past Arnold, which must have come after the presidential limousine passed the Stemmons sign. Those shots may have created the two grooves pointing southeast in the grass on the south side of Elm Street, which indicates that the shooter was elevated, i.e., on the "grassy knoll." In any case, Arnold appears to have heard at least five shots but never reported hearing the explosion of a muzzle blast, just the "crack" of bullets breaking the sound barrier, which points to the use of silencers on several assassin weapons.

When the shooting stopped, Arnold felt a sharp kick and saw standing over him a man in a policeman's uniform, who told him to get up. As Arnold rose to his feet, a second 'policeman' appeared. He was crying and shaking, had no hat, had dirty hands and held a shotgun in his hands, which he waved nervously at Arnold. The 'policemen' demanded Arnold's film. Terrified, Arnold threw his camera to the 'policeman', who pulled the film from the camera and threw it back to Arnold. The two 'policemen' then walked away, leaving Arnold shaken. He ran to his car and drove off. So Arnold met one bogus 'Secret Service' man and two bogus 'policemen.'[70]

Phillip Willis

Willis was with his wife and two young daughters, taking pictures of the motorcade. Willis knew Jack Ruby by sight prior to the assassination and later said, "I also got a photo, taken immediately after [the shots], that shows Ruby standing in front of the Depository building. He was the only person there wearing dark glasses. He was identified by people who knew him."[71]

12:31:08 P.M.

Fifteen seconds after the last shot, even before the presidential limousine had vanished into the underpass, Vicki Adams, at her fourth floor perch, decided she had to go downstairs and find out what had happened. She grabbed her friend Sandra Styles, and the two young women raced across the fourth floor to the rear of the building and clattered down the northwest stairs in their three inch heels, arriving at the first floor about a minute later (which would be 12:32:08), Vicki testified.

An older Black man was standing near the elevators, and Vicki asked him if the President had been shot, but the man did not answer. The two women then continued their run, exiting the building out the back loading door, near the northeast corner of the TSBD.[72]

The sighting of that Black man was odd. The only person he could have been was Troy Eugene West, who later testified he had been seated by his wrapping table, eating his lunch, his back to the elevators. So why did Adams and Styles see him standing near the elevators? Was he waiting for someone to come down in an elevator?

113

He testified that "just after I made coffee, I just had started to eat my lunch…but before I got through, well, all of this was, I mean, the police and things was coming in." [Did you see anyone else on the first floor while you were eating your lunch?] "It wasn't anybody. I didn't see anybody around at that time." [Did you see anyone else on the first floor?] "No, sir; I didn't see." Didn't even see Vicki Adams and Sandra Styles, who spoke to him? Nor any strange men coming down on a freight elevator? His testimony is disingenuous.

The WC later inserted into the transcript of Vicki Adams' testimony, "…and encountered Bill Shelley and Bill Lovelady [instead of West] on the first floor," in an attempt to create a more favorable time line for its claim that Harvey was "a lone nut" – but Vicki always denied that those two men were there, as did Sandra Styles.[73]

Bill Shelley testified on April 7, 1964 that immediately after the shots "…Billy Lovelady and myself took off across the street to that little old island…. Officers started running down to the railroad yards, and Billy and I walked down that way." They didn't return to the building for about five minutes, through a west side door, he testified.

However, previously, on November 22, 1963, Shelley gave an affidavit, in which he stated, "I heard what sounded

114

like three shots…. I ran across the street to the corner of the park & ran into a girl [Gloria Calvery] crying & she said the President had been shot. I went back to the building & went back inside & called my wife & told her what happened. I was on the first floor then & I stayed at the [passenger?] elevator & was told [by Roy Truly] not to let anyone out of the elevator. I left the elevator and went with the police on up to the other floors. I left Jack Dougherty in charge of the elevator." No mention of Billy Lovelady, the jaunt to the rail yards, or coming back through a side door five minutes later. Nor seeing Vicki Adams.

Meanwhile, Vicki and Sandra rushed out the TSBD back door to the Houston Street dock and down some steps near the rear of the dock. Vicki later stated, "At the time I left the building…there was an officer standing about two yards from the curb…and when we were running [from] the dock…he didn't encounter us or ask us what we were doing or where we were going."

Why was that officer just standing there? Most policemen were running toward the "grassy knoll" at that moment. Could he have been waiting for the assassins to come out the back door? And if anyone had challenged them, would he have vouched for them and said they were Secret Service agents? Was he even a real DPD policeman?

115

THE BAKER/TRULY FANTASY ODYSSEY

Before the patently false accounts in the affidavits and later testimonies of TSBD superintendent Roy S. Truly and motorcycle police officer Marion L. Baker are laid out, recall that at the times claimed in their stories, Harvey Oswald was standing on the front steps of the TSBD.

Even the Truly/Baker reports on the first moments of their supposed saga are doubtful. The following appears to refute their claim that they dashed into the TSBD immediately after the shots:

FBI report 3/26/64: "Mrs. [Peggy Joyce] Hawkins stated she stayed behind the restraining wall [with her small child] until she realized there would be no more shots and then walked back to the front of the TSBD building. She said that a motorcycle police officer was in front of the building at this time and that she heard over his [police] radio some remarks about the railroad yards." [The radio transmission probably was Jesse Curry's, in the lead car, who said that immediately after the shots.] "Mrs. Hawkins then reentered the TSBD building by the front door and went upstairs to the third floor *by elevator*." (Yet when Vicki Adams entered the TSBD three or four minutes later both the passenger elevator and the freight elevators were not working, had no power, she said. There is no reason to doubt her.)

"The [NBC cameraman] James Darnell film only shows Baker's run, it does *not* show him going up the steps.... You can see Truly in the Darnell film slowly turning and making his way towards the front steps, but at a slow speed compared to Baker."[74] Frazier and Molina – then standing at the top of the TSBD steps – testified to the WC that they had not seen Baker come up the steps.

That establishes where Truly and Baker were from 12:31 to about 12:32:30. They were outside.

The stories of Truly and Baker changed day by day. The first version was set down by Baker in a handwritten report submitted to the DPD sometime during the early evening of November 22:

"Friday, November 22, 1963 I was riding motorcycle escort for the President of the United States. At approximately 12:30 P.M. I was on Houston Street, and the President's car had made a left turn from Houston onto Elm Street.

"Just as I approached Elm Street I heard three shots. I realized those shots were rifle shots, and I began to try to figure out where they came from. I decided the shots had come from the building on the northwest corner of Elm and

Houston. This building is used by the Board of Education for book storage.

"I jumped off my motor and ran inside the building. As I entered the door I saw several people standing around. I asked these people where the stairs were. A man stepped forward and stated he was the building manager and that he would show me where the stairs were. I followed the man to the rear of the building, and he said, 'Let's take the elevator.' [However], the elevator was hung several floors up, so we used the stairs instead.

"As we reached the third or fourth floor I saw a man walking away from the stairway. I called to the man and he turned around and came back toward me. The manager said, 'I know that man, he works here.' I then turned the man loose and went up to the top floor. The man I saw was a white man approximately 30 years old, 5'9", 165 pounds, dark hair and wearing a light brown jacket."

The weight, hair color and supposed age were that of *Lee* Oswald – who Baker never met on the third or fourth floor. The pictures of Lee in the Marines show him looking five to six years older than his age even then. But how could Truly have mistaken Lee for Harvey? Truly knew Harvey, had hired him, saw him every day. Lee was thirty pounds heavier, had dark hair that receded like a widow's peak – squared off on the back of his neck, was two inches taller, and looked six years older than Harvey. And why would Harvey have put on a windbreaker to go shoot the President?

Further, at 12:45, while Baker and Truly supposedly were checking out the roof of the TSBD, the description of a suspect was broadcast over the police radio: "White male, approximately 30, 165 pounds, slender build." This closely matches Baker's police report. Where did the dispatcher get that description from? Not from Baker.

Plus, before and after Baker's supposed encounter with "Oswald", everyone said "Oswald" (Lee) was wearing just a white T-shirt and "Oswald" (Harvey) a rust-brown long-sleeved shirt, so where did the "light brown jacket" in Baker's report come from? Baker didn't submit his affidavit until late afternoon or early evening of November 22, by which time the "official line" was that "Lee Harvey Oswald" had killed J. D. Tippit, wearing a light-colored windbreaker. It was crucial to tie Harvey to the Tippit murder, so it seems that Baker's report simply followed the "official line." That is, he never saw Harvey. None of that mattered – later that day, Baker identified Harvey as the man he saw at the TSBD.

Skipping past Baker's later account of this incident for

a moment, below is superintendent Truly's affidavit of what took place, submitted in longhand on November 23:

"Mr. O. V. Campbell, one of the owners, and I started to lunch a few minutes after twelve o'clock. We saw that the parade was nearly down to us, so we [stopped] and watched the president go by.

"After the pres. passed, we heard what sounded like an explosion. I heard three such exp. Then I realized they must have been shots. I saw an officer break thru the crowd and go into our building.

"I realized he did not know anything about the bldg. So I ran in with him. The officer and I went through the shipping dept. to the freight elevators. We then started up the stairway. We hit the second floor landing [and] the officer stuck his head into the break room area, where there are Coke and candy machines. Lee Oswald was in there. The officer had his gun on Oswald and asked me if [Oswald] was an employee. I answered yes. We then went up the stairs to the 5th floor, where we found the elevator open.

"We took the elev. to the 7th floor and [then climbed] out on the roof. We searched the roof and a small room [on it]....We did not find anything. We started down on the elevator."[75]

Obviously, the two reports don't match. Notice that Baker said that several people were "standing around." No such thing – *no* people were standing around twenty seconds after the shots, including Truly. Baker then wrote he met a man [doesn't identify the man] *on the third or fourth floor*. Never happened. His description of the man he saw as "a white man approximately 30 years old, 5'9", 165 pounds, dark hair and wearing a light brown jacket" does not describe Harvey, who was 23 years old, weighed 132 pounds, had medium brown hair – with hair growing down his neck, did not own a light brown windbreaker jacket, was wearing a rust-brown tweed shirt all day.

A third version of the event soon appeared. On the morning of November 23rd, *The Dallas Morning News* published a lengthy article by reporter Kent Biffle, who had overheard Truly telling Homicide Captain Will Fritz that he had seen "Oswald" near the small [southeast] storage room, which raises the question of *when* Truly reputedly saw "Oswald." Biffle wrote that, "In a storage room on the first floor, the officer [Marrion Baker], gun drawn, spotted Oswald. 'Does this man work here?' the officer reportedly asked Truly." Truly said he did. Notice that – as in the lunchroom tale – it's again Truly who 'saves' Lee from capture.

121

The story was corroborated several times. Detective Ed Hicks told the *London Free Press* [Toronto] (11/23/63) that *as Oswald came out* "a policeman asked him where he was going. He said he wanted to see what the excitement was all about." The *Sydney Morning Herald* (11/23/63) reported that "Oswald...was stopped by a policeman. Oswald told the policeman that, 'I work here,' and when another employee confirmed that he did, *the policeman let Oswald walk away*." James "Junior" Jarman told the HSCA, "I heard that Oswald had come down through the [second floor] office and came down the front stairs, and he was stopped by the officer....and Mr. Truly told them that was alright, that he worked here, so *then [Lee Oswald] proceeded on out of the building...*." No encounter with Oswald on the fourth floor, third floor, second floor.

Then came the "official" story. On March 25, 1964 Baker testified before the WC– *so he and Truly had had four months after the assassination to polish up their story*. As you read Baker's 'let's pretend' account below, remember that Harvey was standing on the TSBD steps the whole time.

Baker told the WC that he was riding his motorcycle north on Houston Street, sixty feet past Main Street, beside the fourth press car. Seeing a flock of pigeons fly up from the TSBD roof at the first shot, he came roaring down the street, a distance of 180 to 200 feet. He jumped off his bike approximately 45 feet from the doorway of the TSBD, he said, pushed his way through the crowd of people standing outside, and rushed into the building – although TSBD employees Frazier and Molina didn't see him come by them.

Truly saw Baker, ran after him – right past Harvey – into the lobby, told Baker he was the building manager, and the two of them ran to the freight elevators near the northwest corner, they testified – a distance of 80 to 110 feet. Truly did *not* see Shelley and Lovelady there, he said.

Both elevators were stuck on the fifth floor, Truly testified, so he called upstairs, "Real loud....'Turn loose the elevator.'" [And how many times did you yell that?] "Two times....." [Did the elevator come down?] "It did not." So, then, Truly claimed, he rushed up the stairs, Baker following him, gun drawn.

However, Vicki Adams testified, [Did you hear anyone using the stairs?] "No, sir." [Did you hear anyone calling for an elevator?] "No, sir." [Did you see the superintendent of the warehouse, Roy S. Truly?] "No, sir, I did not." [What about any motorcycle police officers?] "No, sir."

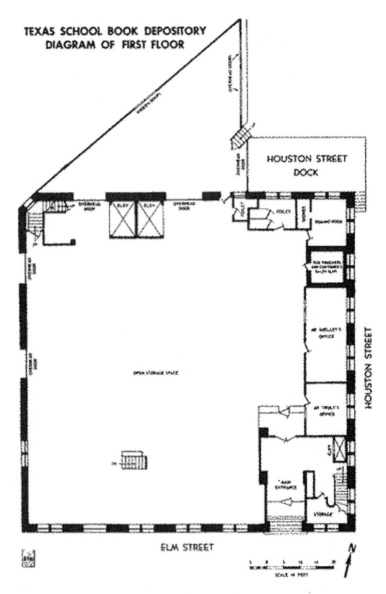

TEXAS SCHOOL BOOK DEPOSITORY
DIAGRAM OF FIRST FLOOR

HOUSTON STREET
DOCK

HOUSTON STREET

ELM STREET

COMMISSION EXHIBIT No. 1061

A big problem with this Baker/Truly account so far is that if it had happened as told they would have reached the stairs about fifty seconds after the first shot, but Vicki Adams and Saundra Styles were still coming down the stairs at that time – and Vicki later told researcher Barry Ernest that she didn't see Truly, Baker, Shelley, Lovelady or Oswald on her way down and out of the building. Keep

The chaotic first floor of the TSBD.

in mind that Vicki had nothing at stake – Truly may very well have.

Also note Baker's immediate recognition of a "rifle shot" and supposedly instantaneous reaction to it, in contrast to virtually everyone else in Dealey Plaza. Most people, including sheriff's deputies, policemen and Secret Service agents – many of them combat veterans or long-time hunters – either didn't realize that the first shot was a rifle report or didn't respond to it.

Truly said he took two or three steps up toward the third floor, realized Baker wasn't following him and returned to the landing. He heard a voice from the

125

lunchroom and, he testified, "saw the officer almost directly in the doorway of the lunchroom facing Oswald – which researchers have written is physically impossible.

Carolyn Arnold had seen Harvey eating in the second floor lunchroom at 12:15. Plus – something most people

TEXAS SCHOOL BOOK DEPOSITORY
DIAGRAM OF SECOND FLOOR
SHOWING ROUTE OF OSWALD

aren't aware of – JFK's motorcade was five minutes late. It had been scheduled to pass the TSBD at 12:25. Why would Harvey be eating in the lunchroom at 12:15 if he intended to shoot JFK at 12:25, and then be in the lunchroom again at 12:32 – *supposedly* now wearing a light brown windbreaker?

Baker continued his testimony, "I caught a glimpse of him and I ran over there and opened that door and hollered at him.... He was *walking away* from me, about 20 feet away from me in the lunchroom...walking east." [...he then walked back toward you?] "Yes, sir." [...anything in his hands?] "He had nothing at that time. [Was he calm and collected?] "Yes, sir. He never did say a word or nothing. In fact, he didn't change his expression one bit.... As I left he was still in the position that he was...."

Baker also was asked, "Do you recall whether or not [Oswald] was wearing the same clothes...in the police station as when you saw him in the lunchroom," and he responded, "Actually, just looking at him, he looked like he didn't have the same thing on." But the WC attorney didn't ask Baker *what* the difference in clothing was.

Truly and Baker testified that they resumed running up the stairs until they got to the fifth floor, from where they took the east elevator to the seventh floor. Why the *east* elevator? Where was the *west* elevator? It supposedly was stuck on the fifth floor. Truly and Baker then "ran up a little stairway that leads out through a little penthouse onto the roof."

Baker said he looked around the roof for several minutes, checking out "some kind of a shack on the northeast corner," but found nothing, so they went back downstairs, they testified. This is the tale Baker and Truly told the WC and wanted the world to believe. Why? To frame Harvey. It wasn't their idea, of course. Probably David Atlee Phillips'.

As noted, "Junior" Jarman had been watching the motorcade on the fifth floor with his two friends. What he next told the WC helps give the lie to the Truly/Baker WC testimony: "[How long was it before you ran to the west end [of the building] from the time of the shots...?"] "After the third shot was fired, I would say it was about a minute...." [And where did you go then?] "We ran to the elevator, *but the elevator had gone down*...." [Which elevator did you run to?] "The elevator on the west side." [On the west. That [elevator] wasn't there?] "No, sir." No one ever said or even asked how or when it went down.

At that time, Truly and Baker were supposedly running up the stairs, and the two elevators were supposedly stuck on the fifth floor. Jarman says nothing about the east elevator. The WC attorney doesn't ask. Jarman and his two friends then *ran down the stairs.* Jarman told the FBI that he did not see a policeman on the stairs, i.e., did *not* meet Truly and Baker coming up the stairs.[76]

So the entire Truly/Baker story (second, third, fourth floor versions) is fiction. Truly and Baker had stopped "Oswald" *on the first floor.* The only "Oswald" inside the TSBD at that moment was Lee, by the storage room. Consequently, if Truly and Baker remained on the first floor, that would have allowed the time and space for the three assassins still upstairs to be taken down a freight elevator by a TSBD employee conspirator.

So the way the four assassins escaped from the sixth floor now becomes clear. No one ever reported hearing any footsteps coming down the back stairs or seeing three men, so the assassins and Lee Oswald *had* to have been taken down in a freight elevator – although the power was said to be off – by TSBD employee Jack Dougherty, who *also took Lee Oswald down at the same time*, let him off at the second floor, and took the other three to the first floor. Vicki Adams reportedly said later that on her way down, she noticed the freight elevator cables were moving.[77]

Lee then quickly entered the lunchroom, bought a Coke[78] from the machine in there, removed the cap from the bottle and sauntered into the north entrance of the second floor offices, just as Mrs. Robert Reid entered the south entrance, at about 12:33. She testified:

"I looked up and Oswald was coming in the back door of the office.... *He had on a white T-shirt* and some kind of wash trousers.... *He did not have any jacket on....* He had gotten a Coke and was holding it in his right hand.... I met him...and I said, "Oh, the President has been shot, but maybe they didn't hit him." He mumbled something to me, I kept walking, he did, too...he was very calm. I thought it was a little strange that one of the warehouse boys would be up in the office.... The only time I had seen him in the office was to come and get change." Asked by the WC how many times she'd seen Oswald since he began working there, she said about five times: "I can't recall seeing him [in the lunchroom] but three times. " So she wasn't very familiar with Harvey's face and build, like Truly was. She didn't even know Oswald's name at the time she encountered him.

Then why was Baker's first account of "Oswald" on the "third or fourth floor" concocted? Simple: it fit the supposed time line of "the lone gunman." So why change the story to the second floor lunchroom? Because Mrs. Reid saw "Oswald" exit the lunchroom around the same time as Baker and Truly supposedly "saw" "Oswald" on the "third or fourth floor." However, Baker, Truly and their handlers weren't aware of Mrs. Reid's observation on November 22, as she wasn't interviewed by the FBI until November 26. Once her account was learned, the story shifted to the second floor lunchroom, to coordinate with Mrs. Reid's statement, even though it made the new

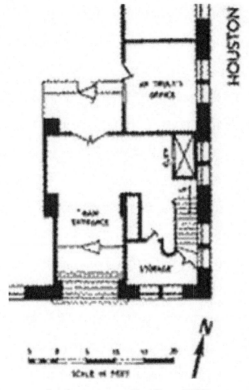

Southeast corner, first floor, TSBD.

"Oswald" time line very tight. Having passed Mrs. Reid, Lee continued walking through the office and down the southeast stairs to the first floor.[79] He ducked into the small storage room beside the steps to put down his Coke bottle. TSBD Vice President O. V. Campbell was then running into the building. He turned right, toward the southeast passenger elevator and stairs, heading for his second floor office. He had just missed running into Lee coming down the stairs.

The next day Campbell was quoted by the *New York Herald Tribune* as saying, "Shortly after the shooting, we raced back into the building.... We saw him [Oswald] in a small storage room on the first floor." Who was "we"? And being Vice President of TSBD, Campbell had seen very little of Harvey, so, like all other witnesses, he thought Lee was Harvey.

This account seems to be the "smoking gun" that shoots down the Truly/Baker lunchroom testimony but raises another question: why did either Truly or Baker even notice Lee on the first floor – and, considering Lee's timeline, the event had to have been right after 12:33, moments after Truly and Baker had actually entered the TSBD.

According to Vicki Adams' supervisor, Dorothy Ann Garner, she saw a policeman come up the stairs to the fourth floor, *after* Vicki and Sandra had gone down. So, although the lunchroom encounter did not take place, perhaps Truly/Baker's climb up the stairs *might* have.

There is one final possibility. What if Baker's supposed dash into the TSBD was not to try to catch a rooftop sniper but to kill "Oswald," and Truly stopped Baker by the storage room only when he saw that the "Oswald" standing there was Lee, not Harvey? Maybe that was Truly's assignment: make sure Baker killed the right "Oswald." Killing "Oswald" just then – 'resisting arrest' – would have wrapped up JFK's murder, closing the case in five minutes, as the plotters hoped.

Accounts of all TSBD employees show that *everyone* but West and Dougherty was either outside or looking out of south-facing windows overlooking Elm Street.[80] Only Vicki and Sandra were immediately in motion after the shots, and they were gone from the building in just over a minute – *never having seen Truly and Baker.* And the only policeman to enter the TSBD right after the shots was Baker.

So then, TSBD employee Dougherty – who had no alibi, was considered suspicious by a WC attorney and testified he rode the west freight elevator to the sixth floor at 12:30 – took Lee and the other three conspirators down on the west freight elevator at around 12:32. Lee walked down the front stairs and was seen by Truly, Baker, Campbell and others, in, or by, the small storage room.

133

And the reason Lee was a shooter in the TSBD was to frame Harvey! Look-alike Lee was <u>meant</u> to be seen – as "Lee Harvey Oswald, the TSBD employee" – and he *was* seen, by at least thirteen people, both inside and outside the TSBD.[81] Simultaneously, Lee's doppelgänger looks allowed him to escape from the TSBD. A brilliant "hall of mirrors" ploy, dreamt up by the CIA renegades. The other three assassins ran out the back door, right past Troy West.

But why did Truly/Baker say they had encountered "Lee Harvey Oswald" upstairs in the TSBD, when Harvey was out front on the steps and Lee was on the first floor in the small storage room? Simple: the plotters didn't want the

The chaotic sixth floor.

"lone nut" to be seen downstairs less than three minutes after the shooting, especially since no one had heard Lee run down the stairs.

The *supposed* timeline of "Oswald" going from the sixth floor *southeast* corner "sniper's nest" to the second floor lunchroom – entrance near the *northwest corner* – was tenuous enough: the sixth floor was filled with tall stacks of boxes full of books. "Oswald" being in the first floor storage room so soon must have seemed untenable to those orchestrating the frame up, so Truly and Baker were told to report "Oswald" in the second floor lunchroom, creating a more believable time line. That's also why the transcript of Vicki's testimony was altered.

In addition, the Truly/Baker lunchroom tale precluded the possibility of shooters other than Oswald, as supposedly the elevators "were stuck" on the fifth floor, so no assassins could have taken one of those down – and since Truly and Baker supposedly were charging up the steps, no one could have come down the steps, either, leaving only "the lone nut" in the lunchroom – which never happened.

12:32:30 P.M.

Richard Randolph Carr, who the WC never saw fit to call, later testified at the New Orleans Clay Shaw trial in 1969 that he saw a Rambler station wagon parked on the wrong side of Houston, facing north, next to the TSBD.

He stated, "Immediately after the shooting there was three men that emerged from behind [the northeast corner of] the School Book Depository. There was a Latin – real dark-complected – stepped out and opened the door; [the first] two men entered that station wagon; and the Latin drove it north on Houston. The car was in motion before the rear door was closed."

The third man, whom Carr had seen in a sixth floor TSBD window earlier, then emerged from behind the TSBD, crossed to the east side of Houston, and walked south "in a very big hurry – every once in a while he would look over his shoulder, as if he was being followed...." Then the man turned left on Commerce Street, heading toward town. "He had on a felt hat, a light hat, he had on heavy-rimmed glasses, dark, heavy ear pieces on his glasses...[and] he had on a tie, ...a light shirt, a tan sport coat."

Asked by District Attorney Jim Garrison if he'd spoken to FBI agents about this incident, Carr said, "Yes, I did." What did they tell him to do? "I done as I was instructed – I shut my mouth," Carr replied.

~

Witness James Worrell saw a man in a sport coat run out of the back of the TSBD. Witnesses had seen a man in a sport coat with a rifle in the sixth floor southeast window of the TSBD prior to the shooting. Worrell also testified he heard four shots, saw the rifle, and that the barrel only extended four inches from its stock, like a Mauser.

~

Harvey was still outside the TSBD, in his rust-brown tweed shirt, just after 12:32 P.M., when a young man about 29 years old ran up to him and asked for a phone. Harvey knew where that phone was – he had been standing next to it at noon. He pointed to the lobby and said, "It's in there." They made brief eye contact, and then the young man ran in. The man was Pierce M. Allman, who was a program director for the Dallas television and radio station WFAA. He needed a phone to call his station, talked on that phone for the next forty minutes, described what was taking place on the first floor of the TSBD.[82] *The Dallas Morning News* reporter Kent Biffle saw him there.

Now Harvey turned left and began to walk east on Elm Street. Less than a minute later, NBC White House correspondent Robert MacNeil ran toward the TSBD, also looking for a phone:

"As I ran up the steps and through the door, a young man in shirt sleeves was coming out. In great agitation I asked him where there was a phone. He pointed inside to an open space where another man was talking on the phone situated near a column and said, 'Better ask him.' I [went] inside and asked the second man [Pierce Allman], who pointed to an office at one side. I found a telephone on the desk [there].... My New York news desk has since placed the time of my call at 12:36."[83]

The young man MacNeil spoke with *had* to have been Lee. Who else would be *leaving* the TSBD *at 12:34 and not know where a phone might be inside?* Employees were not leaving – they were rushing into the building. And the only young white males working in the TSBD that day beside Harvey were Lovelady, Frazier and Lewis. All three were outside then.

When Lee exited the TSBD and came down the steps, Mrs. Velez and her two friends saw Jack Ruby give Lee a handgun. The women were said to know "Lee Harvey Oswald," *who spoke Spanish very well* and who they'd once eaten lunch with at a nearby restaurant. Recall that Jack Ruby's Carrousel Club was only eight blocks southeast of the TSBD. Two of the women were acquainted with Ruby. The women were never interviewed by the FBI.[84]

Lee then walked a short distance west on the Elm Street extension in front of the TSBD and waited.

~

KRLD-TV reporter and future Dallas Mayor Wes Wise saw Jack Ruby walking around the corner of the TSBD a few minutes after the assassination. Some researchers believe that the man with the hat to Harvey's right in Altgens6 was Jack Ruby.[85]

~

Beside the bogus 'Secret Service agents' already noted, there were others. After the shots, DPD policeman Joe M. Smith ran into the parking lot behind the "grassy knoll." There he encountered a man who pulled Secret Service credentials from his hip pocket. Smith had seen such credentials before, so he let the man go, without even enquiring what the 'Secret Service agent' was doing there.

Smith: "He looked like an auto mechanic. He had on a sports shirt and sports pants. He had dirty fingernails…and hands that looked like an auto mechanic's hands…. I should have checked the man closer." He certainly should have – no Secret Service agent ever dressed or looked like that.

Witness Malcolm Summers ran up the slope of the "grassy knoll" and was stopped by a man in a suit, who had an overcoat over one arm. Under the overcoat, Summers saw a gun, and the man told him, "Don't y'all come up here any further. You could get shot…or killed."

Constable Seymour Weitzman rushed behind the picket fence and met men he believed were Secret Service agents.

At about 12:38, police officer D. V. Harkness went to the back of the TSBD and, he testified, "There were some Secret Service agents there. I didn't get them identified. They told me they were Secret Service." They weren't.[86]

There were uniformed policemen all over the "grassy knoll" and behind the picket fence *after* the shots. Deputy Sheriff W. W. "Bo" Mabra ran behind the picket fence and encountered a uniformed policeman who told him, "I don't know what's going on, but there hasn't been a thing move back here in an hour or more because I've been here all that time." Things wrong with that statement: 1) no one saw a policeman behind the fence before the shooting, 2) other people *were seen* behind the fence by witnesses, 3) the DPD said there were no policemen stationed behind the picket fence before the shots.[87] So, who was that policeman?

~

Meanwhile, Vicki Adams and Sandra Styles "went west towards the tracks...approximately two yards within the tracks, and there was an officer standing there, and he said, 'Get back to the building.'" Again, was he a real cop doing his job, another phony cop, or a real cop helping with the cover-up?

Vicki and Sandra started back but went south and east

down the Elm street extension. Sandra went inside, and later stated she "took the elevator to the fourth floor," while Vicki continued to look around outside. She testified she noticed a man, whom she later saw on television, Jack Ruby, standing on the corner of Houston and Elm shortly before she went back into the TSBD, around 12:36.

Vicki finally went inside, pushed the button for the passenger elevator, but, she said, the power was off, so she went up the nearby stairs to the second floor and walked across the building to the freight elevators. "I went into the [west] elevator which was stopped on the second floor, with two men who were dressed in suits and hats, and I assumed they were plainclothesmen." Then she "tried to get the elevator to go to the fourth floor, but it wasn't operating, so the gentlemen lifted the elevator gate and *we* went out...."

Two strange men in suits and hats are standing in a motionless elevator on the second floor? So, who were they, why were they just standing on the elevator, *where did they come from, and where did they go*? This was only 5-6 minutes after the President was shot – how could two plainclothesmen have arrived there so soon? And just standing still on a stopped elevator?

But the WC didn't ask Vicki a single question about

these men! The WC had pinpointed where every TSBD employee was in and around the building but wasn't interested in two strange men standing motionless on a stopped elevator car at 12:36?! And all TSBD employee affidavits state that no one saw any strange men in the TSBD that day. Who had Vicki seen?

Plus, we know that the Truly/Baker elevator story never happened but that the passenger elevator seemingly did work for Sandra Styles. Why didn't the passenger elevator and west elevator work for Vicki? And who had brought the west elevator to the second floor? And why?

~

"Tosh" Plumlee walked through the south knoll area from where he had heard shots and smelled gunpowder. He and his associates were picked up on the back side of the underpass, the southwest side. At about 2:00 p.m. the team took off from Red Bird Airport.

12:40 P.M.

President Kennedy and Governor Connally had been rushed – at over eighty miles an hour – to Parkland Hospital, where they were immediately wheeled into individual trauma rooms. The wounds seen there, as reported, are as follows:

142

President Kennedy

Listed in the most likely order that bullets struck JFK:

1. Throat, entrance wound, frontal shot. A small, neat wound, "clear-cut diameter" of 4-5 mm.[88] Seen by a number of witnesses, including Parkland Hospital doctors.

2. Left temple, downward trajectory, entrance wound, frontal shot. Since the limousine was facing 120^0 (to the left), the shot had to have come from the south knoll to hit JFK in the left temple. Bullet fragments may have lodged in the brain *and* exited through the subsequent egg-shaped hole that was created by this bullet in the lower right rear of JFK's head.

Canadian journalist Norman Similas, who was ten feet from the president, was quoted in *The New York Times*, 11/24/63, "I could see a hole in the president's left temple."[89]

Dr. Marion Jenkins, chief anesthesiologist, Parkland Hospital, "I thought there was a wound on the left temporal area, right at the hairline."[90]

The *St. Louis Post Dispatch* reported on Dec. 1, 1963 that a Dallas doctor had said that the left temporal wound was a small entry wound.[91]

Dr. Adolph Giesecke of Parkland thought he had seen a wound in the left temple.[92]

Dr. Robert McClelland, Parkland Hospital, reported; "Cause of death massive head and brain injury from a gunshot wound of the left temple."[93]

The *Philadelphia Sunday Bulletin,* on November 24, 1963, reported that Oscar Huber, the priest who administered the last rites to JFK, said that the President had "a terrible wound" over his left eye.[94]

The skull was shattered *on the left* cerebral hemisphere, not just the right, reported at Bethesda.[95]

Witness Hugh Huggins: "I distinctly saw an entry wound in the left temple...."[95]

Dr. Gene Akin, Parkland Hospital, "thought he saw a bullet entrance wound on the President's forehead." He considered the wound significant and did not report it at the time "because he did not want to be killed by any conspirators."[96]

Dr. Donald Seldin, Parkland Hospital: "The bullet struck the President in the forehead...the entire frontal, parietal and temporal bones were shattered."[97]

Dr. David Stewart, Parkland Hospital: "there was a small wound in the left front of the President's head...."[98]

Dr. Lito Porto, Parkland Hospital, saw a bullet entry wound near the left temple.[99]

144

An unnamed Secret Service agent "observed a massive wound on the President's left forehead and used his coat to cover the President's head" at Parkland.[99a]

A drawing by autopsy surgeon J. Thornton Boswell, at Bethesda, depicting a top view of JFK's skull, shows a wound in the left forehead.

The autopsy face-sheet – a diagram showing the frontal view of the President's body – has a black dot over the left eye. A black dot was used in the same

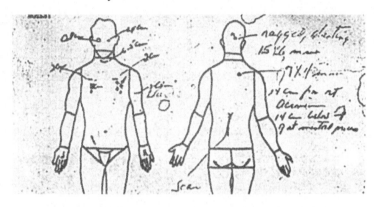

diagram to represent the other wounds on the body (see diagram above).[100]

3. Back of the head, rear shot. Missile entered into the same area as the egg-shaped exit wound, may have lodged in the brain but no entrance or exit wound seen.

James Files. Just as he pulled the trigger of his pistol, JFK's head lurched forward from a rear shot.

Zapruder film, each frame 1/18 of a second. One frame shows JFK's head move forward two inches, followed immediately by a violent head motion backward and to the left.[101] That corroborates Files' account, demonstrates a rear shot.

4 & 5. Right side of the head, two entrance wounds, to the front and side.

Secret Service Agent Sam Kinney saw one shot strike the right side of JFK's head.[102]

Motorcycle officer B. M. Hargis: rode to the left and rear of JFK, said the fatal shot struck the right side of the President's head.[103]

Witness Abraham Zapruder said JFK was hit in the right temple.

Witness Bill Newman said a shot struck in the right temporal area.[104]

Texas Highway Patrolman Hurchel Jacks, at Parkland Hospital, saw that the fatal bullet "had struck [JFK] above the right ear or near the [right] temple."[105]

Witness Marilyn Sitzman, who stood beside Abraham Zapruder, said a bullet "struck JFK in the right temporal area, above the ear and to the front...between the eye and the ear."[106]

Motorcycle Officer Douglas L. Jackson "witnessed JFK hit above the right ear and the top of his head 'exploded.'"[106a,]

Shooter James Files hit JFK above his right eye with an explosive bullet.

Maryland medical examiner Russell S. Fisher, who reviewed JFK autopsy photos and X-rays for Attorney General Ramsey Clark in 1968, later told a researcher, "The bullet that hit JFK in the head disintegrated completely. We saw nearly 40 fragments throughout the *right cerebral hemisphere* and imbedded in the interior of the skull." Fisher also found a bullet fragment "near the entrance in JFK's head" imbedded in the skull from the outside, which may have been a ricochet of a shot that missed.[107]

Speculation must be brought into play now, due to the two differing accounts: one, that the bullet struck JFK's right temple or right forehead, the second, that the bullet hit above his right ear. As those two areas on JFK's head are three to four inches apart, could witnesses have been reporting two wounds, not just one?

Note that James Files said he aimed for JFK' right eye, but that a bullet from behind JFK, a fraction of a second earlier, pushed his head forward. As there was at least one specific and credible report of a bullet hole above JFK's right eye,[107a] that would seem to be Files' shot.

Further, several researchers strongly maintain that there was a shooter in a storm drain to the front and right of the presidential limousine and that the shooter fired the fatal shot to the right side of JFK's head. It has been claimed that the shooter in the storm drain was mobster Johnny Roselli. If so, he was the eighth shooter.

Newsman Sam Pate 'saw the presidential limousine slow down as it came to the curve in front of the grassy knoll. Then he observed a puff of smoke come from the storm sewer....

'Pete Lucas came up to Pate and told him that the man who killed President Kennedy had gotten away. Lucas went on to say that the assassin's name was Bruno (aka Johnny Roselli), that he was short and stocky, and that he had been positioned in the storm sewer and 'blew Kennedy away with a .45 automatic.'[107b]

The placement of the wounds and the locations of the shooters match. Scientific analysis of the bullet to the right side of JFK's head establishes that the missile came from the right, with an upward trajectory, i.e., Roselli's shot, whereas Files' shot, straight ahead but slightly right, hit

JFK in the right forehead.

All of this leads to the conclusion that *two* shots hit JFK on the right side of his head, one shot fired by Roselli, the other shot by Files—the exploding bullet that blew apart JFK's head. Since it seems that all shots that day were fired in volleys, it is reasonable to think that two or more shots in the third volley hit JFK almost simultaneously. Therefore, it would appear that four shots hit JFK's head: two on the right, one on the left forehead, and one from behind.

6. Rear right lower quadrant of the head, egg-shaped hole, frontal shot from the south knoll—the exit wound of the left temple shot.

Sixteen Dallas doctors and three nurses described seeing this wound.[108] Six of those doctors testified that this large wound in the back of the head was an exit wound.[109]

Secret Service agent Clint Hill, who ran to the presidential limousine and jumped on the back, testified, "The right rear portion of his head was missing. It was lying in the rear seat of the car."

6. Suspected chest wound(s), possibly from shrapnel, possible damage to the top of the right lung.[110]

Several Parkland doctors believed there was chest damage,[111] including Dr. Marion Jenkins, who in his written report noted that JFK had chest damage.[112]

At Parkland a tube was inserted into JFK's chest just below the nipples for drainage[113] If there was no chest damage, why was this done? In fact, what was the tube inserted *into*?

Also notice on the autopsy face-sheet the strange markings above both of JFK's nipples, which must indicate damage to the body.[114] *No* Dallas medical personnel, including those who washed blood off JFK's body, reported seeing a back wound.[115]

Not one of Parkland doctors and nurses in Dallas saw a small entrance wound below the large egg-shaped wound on the back of JFK's head, lower right side.[116]

Governor Connally

A through and through bullet wound from his right armpit to his right nipple, damaging his right lung and shattering his fifth rib; a shattered right wrist, with bullet fragments lodging in it and in his left thigh.

Connally, and his wife, always maintained that he was hit by an entirely different bullet from the one that hit JFK, which fragmented, with two large pieces surgically removed, one falling to the floor, making a sound similar to that of a wedding ring, accordingly to Connally.

Dr. Frederick W. Light, a U.S. Army wound ballistics expert, reported in April, 1964 that Connally was struck by two bullets from behind.[117].

~

Meanwhile, at 12:40 p.m., coming slowly west on Elm street, a light green Nash Rambler station wagon with a chrome luggage rack on top and an out-of-state license plate suddenly pulled over to the north curb and stopped before the TSBD.

Deputy Sheriff Roger Craig, on the south side of Elm Street, heard a shrill whistle and saw a young man wearing a white T-shirt run to the car and get in. The driver of the station wagon was a husky-looking Latin, with dark wavy hair, *wearing a tan windbreaker jacket*, Craig said. This appeared to be the same vehicle and driver that had whisked away two of the TSBD assassins.

Two men in cars behind the Rambler also observed the young man entering the car. Witness Helen Forrest saw the man run to the Rambler and get in. She later said, "If it wasn't Oswald, it was his identical twin." The young man was Lee Oswald, of course. The Rambler then quickly

151

drove west under the triple overpass, heading toward the Oak Cliff section of Dallas.

Craig decided to report this, so he crossed Elm Street and went to a command post that had been set up outside the TSBD. There a man in a gray suit told him, "I'm with the Secret Service." The man, however, showed little interest in Craig's observations, except for the Rambler station wagon. Later in the afternoon Craig went to police headquarters and identified Harvey as the man he had seen.

~

After leaving the TSBD at 12:33, Harvey had walked five blocks east on Elm Street (about four-tenth of a mile), when he saw a "Marsalis" bus stopped in traffic. "He come up and beat on the door of the bus...about even with Griffin Street," bus driver Cecil J. McWatters later testified. He let Harvey on, Harvey paid his fare and went to sit on the second cross seat on the right. It was 12:40, bus driver McWatters firmly stated.

Although Harvey apparently didn't notice her, a former landlady of his, Mrs. Mary Bledsoe, was sitting at the front of the bus, opposite the driver. She testified to the WC that Harvey was wearing "a brown shirt....hole in his sleeve, right elbow...all the buttons torn off.... Shirt open.... Pants ...were gray, and they were all ragged...at the waist." The

WC later showed Mrs. Bledsoe the shirt Harvey had on when arrested, and she insisted it was the shirt he was wearing on the bus. The WC counsel bent over backwards trying to make her say it was another brown shirt, but she stuck to her identification: "That is it…. Yes, it is the shirt." So Harvey didn't change his shirt when he got to his room, as the WC later tried to claim.

Meanwhile, Harvey's bus just crawled along, so when a woman asked to get off two blocks later, near Poydras Street, Harvey asked for a transfer and got off too. But a block further something strange happened with that bus stuck in traffic: a policeman told the driver the president had been shot and said no one was to leave the bus until officers talked to the passengers. Then two policemen boarded the bus and checked each passenger for weapons.

Why? Was every bus in a four-block radius around Dealey Plaza stopped and checked for weapons? And the bus was going *toward* Dealey Plaza, not away from it, fifteen minutes after the shooting. Why would an assassin take a bus? Back past the scene of the crime? Carrying a handgun? What kind of sense does that make?

But the plotters knew Harvey would take this bus because they'd told him to go home. If the cops had found Harvey on the bus, they could have killed him, dropping a "throw-down" handgun, claiming self-defense. Think about it – Harvey had already been set up as the patsy – this was the second opportunity to eliminate him and close the case. There would be three more setups to kill him in the next hour.

Harvey decided to get a taxi, so he went back to Lamar, turned right and walked to the Greyhound Bus Depot, at the northwest corner of Jackson and Lamar – four blocks. Now, consider: Harvey was at the Greyhound Bus Depot. Why didn't he just catch a bus out of town if he was the assassin? Why would he go back to his room? If he was this vicious killer, why did he leave almost all of his cash for Marina? What could he do with only $16 in his pocket?

12:45 P.M.

Lee Oswald and his husky Latin companion drove west on North Zangs Blvd. and at about 12:45 turned left onto North Marsalis Ave. and headed south toward Jefferson Blvd., probably turned left, then continued down Lancaster.

~

Police Officer J. D. Tippit pulled into the Gloco Gas Station (1502 North Zangs, on the southwest corner of the intersection with Marsalis Ave., about 1.5 miles from the TSBD) at 12:45 and parked his squad car facing east. He had been given no orders to be there, in fact was not

154

supposed to be in Oak Cliff at all. He intently watched traffic coming west across the Houston Viaduct onto Zangs Blvd. The "Marsalis" bus had a stop right across the street from the Gloco station that Tippit could observe.

Photographer Al Volkland and his wife were driving by. They knew Tippit, recognized him and waved. Three Gloco employees also knew Tippit. They recalled he was there in his squad car for about ten minutes.[118]

Based on his actions in the subsequent fifteen minutes, Tippit could only have been on the lookout for either Lee or Harvey. But Lee had driven right by the Gloco station at 12:45 and the "Marsalis" bus was stuck in traffic on Elm Street.

~

Harvey got into a taxi at about 12:48. Driver William Wayne Whaley testified to the WC on March 12, 1964: "He was walking south on Lamar...on the west side of the street.... He opened the front door... and got in. He was dressed in just ordinary work clothes.... [His pants] were khaki material...faded blue color. Then he had on a brown shirt with a little silverlike stripe on it... His shirt was open three buttons down. He had on a T-shirt.

"About that time an old lady, I think she was an old lady, I don't remember nothing but her sticking her head

155

down past him in the door and saying, 'Driver, will you call me a cab?' She had seen him get this cab and wanted one, too, and he opened the door a little bit like he was going to get out and said, 'I will let you have this one,' and she says, 'No, the driver can call me one.' I didn't call one because I knew one would come around the block before I could call." Now, what kind of mad assassin gets in a taxi for a getaway, then offers to get out of it for an old lady?

Harvey told Whaley to take him to the 500 block of North Beckley. Harvey's boarding house was at 1026 North Beckley. Why would Harvey want to drive five blocks past his residence? Recall, Harvey had been trained as a spy. He drove by his residence to check if anyone was lying in wait for him. Remember, he expected to be killed this day.

Whaley left the Greyhound Depot at 12:48 and five minutes later, on Zangs Blvd., drove right past Tippit.

1:00 P.M.

After twenty frantic minutes of treatment at Parkland Hospital, JFK was pronounced dead at 1:00 P.M. Despite Gov. Connally's grave wounds, he survived.

~

Whaley's later WC transcripts repeatedly have him testifying that he'd dropped Harvey off in the 500 block of

North Beckley (just as he'd also sworn in his November 23 affidavit), although the WC – trying to shorten the time when Harvey arrived at 1026 – claimed Whaley had dropped Harvey off in the 700 block,

Whether in the 700 block or the 500 block, Harvey exited the cab, crossed to the east side of the street and walked back toward 1026, checking if anyone was following him or waiting for him around his rooming house.

1026 North Beckley Avenue (left), in later years.

Reaching 1026 Harvey turned right and hurried into the house. The housekeeper, Earlene Roberts, stated in an affidavit on December 5, 1963: "At approximately 1:00 P.M. I was sitting in the living room...when...Lee Harvey Oswald came in the front door." On December 9, 1963, Roberts told FBI agents Will Griffin and James Kennedy that "she could not furnish the exact time that Oswald returned. A rough guess would be 1:00 P.M." When she came before the WC on April 8, 1964 some things had become blurred or changed. Asked when Harvey had come in, Roberts said, "Now, it must have been around 1 o'clock, *or maybe a little after ....what time I wouldn't want to say because – "* [The WC lawyer quickly interrupted her.]

"He come in, and I just looked up and I said, 'Oh, you are in a hurry....' He didn't say nothing – he wouldn't say nothing – period.... *Oswald did not have a jacket...*and I don't recall what type of clothing he was wearing. He went on to his room and stayed about three or four minutes."

While in his room, Harvey changed his pants and shoes but kept his brown shirt on. Into his pants pockets he put his wallet, some change and fourteen dollars in paper money, and a key for a P.O. Box. He also put in a pocket a small white box top with the name "Cox's, Fort Worth" and a paycheck stub from American Bakeries (which stub, it was later found, had once been attached to a check made out to one James Jackson, a real person), dated August 22, 1960 – when Harvey was in Russia.[119] Seemingly trash, but…maybe not. He still had in his shirt pocket the bus transfer given to him by bus driver McWatters, indicating he didn't change his shirt.

The WC later claimed Harvey had a loaded pistol and nine loose bullets in his pockets at this time. It will be shown that he didn't. He owned no rifle, pistol, holster or bullets.

Roberts testified that just after Harvey had come in, she heard two beeps of a car's horn, and when she "just glanced out" her *front window*, she saw a black police car. Roberts told FBI agents Griffin and Kennedy that she saw police car #207 in front of her house with two uniformed men in it. "And then…they just went on around the corner [of Zangs]." Further in her testimony she said, "[The car] stopped directly in front of my house…and *I went to the door* and looked…." The Dallas Police Department was never able to determine who those men were.

Roberts continued, "Oswald [was in] his room…only a very few minutes before coming out. I noticed he had a jacket he was putting on. I recall the jacket was a dark color, and it was the type that zips up the front. He was

159

zipping the jacket up as he left."

It has to be noted that Roberts was a suspect witness, had been harassed by the authorities. She also was continually led by WC counsel when testifying. Her testimony, at best, is chaotic, vague or indefinite. There is no proof that Oswald owned such a jacket and no jacket like that was found between this time or afterward. In fact, the WC said Harvey had worn – and had discarded after supposedly killing Tippit – a light-colored windbreaker jacket. No one ever saw Harvey in a dark windbreaker jacket.

Roberts: "Oswald went out the front door. A moment later I looked out the window. I saw Lee Oswald standing on the curb at the bus stop just to the right and on the same side [*east side*] of the street as our house. Just glanced out the window that once. I don't know how long Lee Oswald stood at the curb, nor did I see which direction he went when he left there." This does not sound like natural speech, more like a statement composed by an FBI agent.

However, WC XXII:160 states that "*Several minutes later*, Mrs. Roberts looked out the front window and saw Lee Oswald by the bus stop on Beckley." *Not*, "a moment later."

Roberts subsequently made two comments to the WC:

"I want you to understand that I have been put through the third degree, and it's hard to remember," also said, "Well, you know, I can't see too good how to read. I'm completely blind in my right eye." For an older lady, it certainly was hard to remember information fed to her by FBI agents.

Then, "[You were working there...last fall – 1963?] "Yes, to my sorrows." [Why to your sorrows?] "Well, he was registered as O. H. Lee, and I come to find out he was Oswald – and I wish I had never known it." [Why?] "Well, they put me through the third degree." [Who did?] "The FBI, Secret Service, [Captain] Will Fritz's men and [Sheriff] Bill Decker's." But that's not all. "I had worked for some policemen and sometimes they come by and tell me something that maybe their wives would want me to know...." So, she was friendly with two Dallas cops, too – and what are friends for except to be friendly? Much of her testimony is suspect.

A reading of the various depositions and WC testimonies of Whaley and Roberts makes one's head spin. There is no question that both witnesses had been bullied and manipulated in order to shave off a couple of minutes, trying to get Harvey earlier to the scene of the murder of Officer Tippit.

Bottom line: Harvey arrived wearing his rust-brown

tweed shirt and left with it still on – no zipped jacket, certainly no light-brown windbreaker. He probably arrived at 1:01, reached the bus stop at about 1:05, stood there for a minute or two before being picked up by police car #207.[120]

Just thirty minutes after Harvey left, three Dallas policemen came by, and Roberts let them into Harvey's room. This address wasn't on file with the TSBD – how did the police get it? As they were searching his room, two FBI agents arrived. The policemen and agents took away everything in the room that belonged to Harvey, including his clothes, Roberts stated.

The WC lawyer told Roberts that "[Oswald] **_might_** *have had a pistol or a revolver,*" to which Roberts replied that she hadn't seen and had never known about a gun in Harvey's room. However, after the police searched Harvey's room, she testified, they *supposedly* came out with a holster that she'd never seen before. Which means nothing, as the FBI agents could have brought the holster into Harvey's room. What they did not find were loose bullets or a box that contained either rifle or pistol bullets— a careless oversight by the plotters.

~

Officer Tippit left the Gloco station rapidly and headed south on Marsalis. At 12:54 P.M. he radioed his position as

Lancaster and 8th Street." He turned right onto Jefferson, then drove to the Top Ten Record Store, 338 West Jefferson, a block and a half west of the Texas Theatre, on the south side of Jefferson, near Bishop Street.

Top Ten Record Shop, Bishop Street at right.

He parked his car on Bishop, hurriedly entered the store and asked to use the store's phone. While his number kept ringing, Tippit said nothing, finally hung up the phone, looking stressed. Why the phone call? It certainly wasn't police business – Tippit's radio was working fine. What did he want to ask, or report? And to whom?

Tippit hurried out to his squad car and drove across Jefferson, then one block north on Bishop, turned right on Sunset and left on Zangs. When he saw a car heading west on 10th Street cross Zangs, he turned left on 10th behind it. James A. Andrews later said he was driving west on West 10th Street, just after 1:00 P.M., when a police car suddenly

163

passed him and cut in front of his car at an angle and stopped, forcing him to brake.

Harvey, Lee and Tippit, at about 1:02 P.M.

The police officer jumped out of his car, motioned for Andrews to stay put, then ran back to Andrews' car and looked in the space between the front and back seats. Perplexed, Andrews noted the officer's nameplate, which read "Tippit." Tippit seemed very upset and agitated, Andrews said, and was "acting wild." Without saying a word, Tippit returned to his car and drove off rapidly.[121]

Tippit must have made a U-turn, then crossed Beckley – right after the time Harvey entered his rooming house. But why was Tippit concerned about 10th Street? What did he hope or expect to find on 10th? Of all the streets in Oak Cliff, *why this one? He had to have a reason, a need. Who was he looking for – on that street?* He hadn't been radioed to search for any suspect. *Who* was he after, if not "Lee Harvey Oswald?"

The WC asked three senior Dallas police officers if they could explain Tippit's movements. Not only could none of them offer a reasonable explanation, but none of them was even aware that the dispatcher *supposedly* ordered Tippit to the Oak Cliff neighborhood. Tippit wasn't ordered to Oak Cliff, so what was he doing there?

~

Shortly after 1:00, a barber at 620 East 10th Street, on the south side of the street, just west of Lancaster, saw Lee pass by his shop, heading west *in a great hurry*. The barber believed it was "Lee Harvey Oswald." Harvey was at his rooming house at that time. Lee hurried past the Town and Country Cafe at 604 East l0th, crossed Marsalis Avenue (one block west of Lancaster), and continued west. A minute or two later, William Lawrence Smith, walking east toward the Town and Country Cafe for lunch, said he was sure the man who walked by him was "Lee Harvey Oswald." Harvey was still in his rooming house at that time.

165

Another WC witness, William Arthur Smith, who said he saw Lee walking west, described him as "a white male...150-160 lbs....dark hair...wearing a white shirt, *light brown jacket and dark pants.*" Where was Lee going? Had he been headed straight to the Texas Theatre, he most likely would have walked west on Jefferson Avenue rather than west on East 10th Street. In fact, why wasn't he just dropped off at the Texas Theatre by his driver?

As Lee got near Patton, Tippit, driving east on East 10th, saw Lee – and apparently found who he was looking for because he slowly pulled over close to the curb by Lee, who casually walked over to the squad car and began speaking with Tippit through the passenger side vent window. This was in front of 410 East 10th. Although Lee put his hands on the patrol car, *supposedly* no fingerprints were recovered. One witness said it seemed as if Tippit and Lee knew each other. Recall that Lee and Tippit had been seen at the same time at the Dobbs House Restaurant two mornings earlier.

When Tippit got out of his squad car and started walking forward, Lee drew the pistol he had been given at the TSBD by Jack Ruby and fired across the hood, striking Tippit three times in the chest. As Tippit fell, Lee started to leave, still heading west, but then went around the car to

Tippit and put a fourth bullet into Tippit's head.[122] As Lee ran away, one witness heard him mutter, "Poor dumb cop."

There was a witness, Mrs. Donald Higgins, at 417 East 10th Street, who was *not* called by the WC – for obvious reasons. She heard three or four shots that day, then some screaming, ran to her front door, saw a policeman lying in the street and a man with a gun running toward Patton Street.

Asked in March of 1968 by assassination researcher Barry Ernest when all this began happening, Mrs. Higgins said a moment after 1:06. How was she so sure? She was watching television, and the newscaster turned to look at the clock behind him and said it was six minutes after one, right before the shots. That certainly was not what the WC wanted to hear, so Mrs. Higgins wasn't asked to testify.

Witness Helen Markham, heading to work as a waitress at the same time as she did each day, left her home at 328 East Ninth Street "a little after 1:00," going to catch her regular 1:15 bus at Patton and Jefferson. She had walked about one block south on Patton, to the northwest corner of Patton and East 10th, when she saw the shooting. Asked about the time, she said, "I wouldn't be afraid to bet it wasn't 6 or 7 minutes after 1:00."

Witness T. F. Bowley, who arrived *after* the shooting,

stated that he "...saw a police officer lying next to the left front wheel. I looked at my watch, and it said 1:10 P.M. Several people were at the scene.... The police arrived and...I told him I did not witness the shooting." *Several people* already at the scene would put the shooting not later than 1:06-1:07 *P.M.*

There is no reason to conclude that Tippit was shot later than 1:06, when Harvey was standing outside his rooming house. The WC claimed Tippit was shot at 1:16. However, Bowley grabbed the mike in Tippit's squad car and at 1:16 radioed that a policeman had been shot.

So, Harvey was not there, couldn't have been there, did not shoot Tippit, and the whole case against him was/is bogus. He was framed.

Next, a description of the killer and his clothes by some of the witnesses:

William W. Scoggins: [...what kind of trousers...?] "They was dark, not too dark, and he had on a light shirt.... a pistol in his *left hand.*" Lee was left-handed.

Helen Markham: "He had these dark trousers on....a short jacket open in the front, kind of a grayish tan."

Virginia Davis: "I think [his trousers] were black. Brown jacket...."

Barbara J. Davis: [...a shirt...Commission Exhibit No.

150] "The shirt he had on was lighter than that." [Color of his hair?] "Either dark brown or black. It was just dark hair." [Color of his clothes?] "He...had on dark trousers, and a light colored shirt, with a dark coat over it."

Ted Callaway: "...dark trousers and a light tannish gray windbreaker jacket..., fair complexion, dark hair..., about 5'10"." [...a jacket here, Commission's Exhibit No. 162.] "That is the same type jacket...it had a little more tan to it.... He looked to me like around 160 pounds.... Just a nice athletic type...."

Domingo Benavides: The killer was 5'10" to 5'11", and "I remember the back of his head...looked like his hairline sort of went square instead of tapered off. And he looked like he needed a haircut for about two weeks, but his hair didn't taper off, it kind of went down and *squared off* and made his head look flat in back." Lee Oswald got haircuts like that. Harvey's hair, as can be seen in that day's pictures, was not squared off, in fact was grown down his neck.

Also recall motorcycle officer Marrion L. Baker's description: "A white man, approximately 30 years old, 5'9", 165 pounds, dark hair, wearing a light brown jacket."

However, it was Mrs. Higgins who put the last nail in the coffin to bury the notion that Harvey had shot Tippit, for when Barry Ernest asked her if the man she saw was Lee Harvey Oswald, she answered with a sigh, "He definitely was not the man they showed on television."

As with almost everything that happened this day, questions arose about the weapon that killed Tippit. Based on the shell casings first found on the scene, the weapon was reported to be a .38 caliber automatic pistol, which shortly morphed into a .38 caliber revolver.

The history of the ammunition used in it is even more bizarre, for of the discarded casings supposedly found at the scene two were made by Winchester-Western and two by Remington-Peters, while the bullets removed from Tippit were three Winchester-Western and one Remington-Peters. And, later, five Winchester-Western bullets *supposedly* were found in Harvey's pockets.[123] So, according to the WC, Harvey had fifteen rounds made by two different manufacturers with him when he supposedly shot Tippit.

But where did those rounds come from? Bullets are sold by the box, not by the round. So, where were the rest of the bullets and their two boxes? There were no loose rounds or boxes of pistol (or rifle) bullets found in Harvey's room, nor was it ever discovered where Harvey supposedly had bought ammunition. And why two manufacturers?

To complete the mess, the FBI reported that it was unable to show that any of the bullets had come from any of the casings or from the revolver Harvey supposedly owned. And none of the empty casings or live rounds had Oswald's fingerprints on them. Finally, a DPD policeman was unable to identify for the WC two of the casings that he had handled at the scene, for his initials that he had scratched on two casings were not on the casings he was shown by the WC.

To continue with the event, when Lee got near Patton, he cut across the grass of the corner house, reportedly ejecting the four spent casings from his weapon – which was a very odd thing to do. Having just murdered a policeman, the killer drops four pieces of evidence? Or were the casings dropped deliberately, meant to frame Harvey Oswald? And no one saw Lee reload, which would have been a minor juggling feat: running, pulling loose rounds from the nine in his pocket, reloading on the run, one bullet at a time.

Lee continued on the east side of Patton, then ran across to the west side, still with the gun in his hand. He turned right on East Jefferson Avenue, slipped the gun into his pants at his waist and slowed to a walk.[124.]

171

As he got to Ballew's Texaco Service Station, one block west, at Jefferson and Crawford Streets, on the northeast corner of Jefferson, he ran – north – behind the station and was last seen in the parking lot directly in back of the station, probably continuing west in the alley behind the parking lot, heading toward the Texas Theatre.

A windbreaker jacket, supposedly belonging to the killer – described variously as light grey or white or light brown, was *supposedly* found under a car in the Ballew parking lot by an *unidentified* policeman a little later. The jacket was a "medium" size – Harvey wore "small", but remember Lee's driver: "a husky-looking Latin…*wearing* a tan windbreaker jacket" – and the jacket's laundry and dry cleaning tags couldn't be traced to any laundry or cleaning establishment in the Dallas or New Orleans areas – because if it *was* Lee's or the Rambler driver's, they both had lived in Miami. And Marina had always *washed* Harvey's clothes, as noted earlier.

Next is 'Harvey's' wallet, which mysteriously appeared and disappeared at the Tippit murder scene. *Supposedly*, the killer handed his *entire* wallet to Tippit through the *rolled down* passenger window – despite the fact that witness Virginia Davis said the passenger window was *rolled up*, despite the Dallas police homicide report (below), despite

172

POLICE DEPARTMENT   ...OIDE REPORT   CITY OF DALLAS

Name of Person Killed	First Name	Middle Name	Race	Sex	Age	Residence of Person Killed	Officers Serial No.
TIPPITT, J. D.			w	m/34		238 Glencairn CA4229	F 85827

Reported By: Bus: Police Officer #884 City of Dallas   RI 89711

MURDER

| 400 blk E. Tenth | | | R | 2 | 108 | C. E. Talbert 463 | |
| Fri | 11-22-63 | 1:18pm | | 11-22-63 | 1:8pm | Cave | 5pm—same |

DESCRIPTION OF DEAD PERSON

Judge Joe B Brown Jr.

Dr. Liguori Methodist Hospital DOA at 1:30pm

Deceased driving Squad Car #10 east on Tenth stopped to interrogate a suspect who was walking west on Tenth. Suspect walked to Officer's car on the right hand side, they talked through the closed window for a few seconds. Deceased got out of the car and started to walk around the front of the car to suspect, as he reached the hood of car suspect started shooting striking deceased once in the right temple, once in right side of chest and once in center of stomach. Suspect ran south on Patton from location toward Jefferson. Suspect was later arrested in the balcony of the Texas Theatre at 231 W. Jefferson. Suspect's gun a 38 Special was recovered and turned over to Homicide Bureau. Deceased taken to Methodist Hospital by Dudley-Hughes ambulance and pronounced DOA at 1:30pm by Dr. Liguori, 'udge Joe B. Brown, Jr ordered autopsy. ...... to Parkland Hospital.... Next of Kin .... Notified. Personal effects placed in property room.

"...they talked through the closed window...."

the police photographs of the patrol car, showing the window *rolled up.*

But who hands their entire wallet to a police officer, anyway? And why? A policeman wouldn't make such a request – he wouldn't want to be responsible for the contents of someone's wallet. And a killer so thoughtless that he forgets about the wallet he handed to a policeman moments before he shot him to death?

At around 1:15 P.M. an ambulance was dispatched from the Dudley Hughes Funeral Home and arrived at 10th and Patton within a minute. Dallas Police Reserve Sergeant Kenneth H. Croy testified he arrived at the Tippit murder scene as the ambulance was picking up Tippit's body. So, Croy arrived at the earliest at 1:17. Croy told an interviewer that *an unknown man handed him 'Oswald's' wallet right after his arrival*. Why didn't Croy immediately radio in the

Police Captain W. R. Westbrook holding the wallet.

names on the IDs in the wallet? This was the murder of a policeman, after all, with the killer still running loose.

Ted Callaway and other citizen witnesses responded to the scene. None of them saw a wallet on the ground. Callaway later said, *"There was no billfold on the scene. If there was, there would have been too many people who would have seen it."* The wallet could only have been *brought to the scene* by someone. The wallet was photographed by a TV cameraman, *at 1:42.* What did Sergeant Croy do with the wallet – *supposedly* handed him by "an unknown man" – between 1:17 and 1:42, twenty-five minutes? And where did that wallet go after 1:42? No one could say. Nor did the WC ask Sgt. Croy about the wallet. Why not? A police detective was supposedly talking with an FBI agent about the wallet at the time it was photographed. For years, that FBI agent gave a tortured cock and bull story about the wallet.

The wallet was a "throw-down" to frame Harvey, just as police have used throw-down guns to frame people. It was to provide quick identification of Harvey, so he'd be tied to the Tippit murder immediately. The wallet was there in case he wasn't caught at the Texas Theatre a half hour later. When Harvey was arrested at the theatre, *with a wallet*, the Tippit scene wallet 'vanished.' That wallet *supposedly* contained two IDs, one *supposedly* for Lee Harvey Oswald, the other *supposedly* for Alek J. Hidell. No Dallas cop ever wrote a report about this magical appearing and disappearing wallet.

That's what happed, but considering Tippit's odd and turbulent behavior in the minutes before his death, it seems probable that something different was *supposed* to happen – if Harvey wasn't killed in the TSBD – and what went wrong. Harvey had been told to take a bus home after he left the TSBD and meet his intelligence handler at the

Texas Theatre by 1:10. Tippit may have been ordered to apprehend and kill Harvey when Harvey got off the bus at Zangs Blvd. and Marsalis Ave.

But when traffic got heavy, Harvey left the bus, which prevented him from being shot on the bus – the second opportunity to kill him. When Harvey didn't arrive on the "Marsalis" bus, that eliminated the third chance to kill him – if he'd gotten off the bus there. When Tippit finally saw 'Lee Harvey Oswald,' he wasn't careful enough and was killed.

Now, if "Oswald" wasn't slated to be killed on 10th Street, why was Tippit on that specific street and why did he stop Lee? There just isn't any other logical reason. It's ridiculous to believe Tippit stopped Lee thinking he was a suspect in JFK's murder. The description broadcast was too vague – if Tippit had even heard it – and what would JFK's "lone nut" killer be doing on 10th Street in Oak Cliff? It certainly would stretch credulity past belief to think Tippit meeting Lee was a coincidence.

The mystery of Tippit's actions and his death has never been solved and probably never will, but one fact is certain: Harvey was not present when Tippit was killed. He was standing in front of his rooming house.

~

THE MORPHING RIFLE

Meanwhile, at 1:00 P.M., Dallas police were filmed removing a rifle from the roof of the TSBD. The rifle had no sling, no scope, and the barrel protruded at least 7-8 inches past the stock. In the film, two officers were seen standing on a fire escape at the seventh floor of the Depository, gesturing toward the roof. Then the film showed the rifle being examined.[125]

A few minutes after 1:00, *Fort Worth Star-Telegram* reporter Thayer Waldo watched a group of high-ranking officers huddle together for a conference at the TSBD. When he later spoke with a police secretary who knew about the officers' conversations, she told him they'd found a rifle "on the roof of the School Book Depository."[126] The rifle was never seen again, never mentioned. It must have been on the roof the whole time Baker and Truly supposedly were up there.

At 1:22 Deputy Constable Seymour Weitzman found a 7.65 German Mauser bolt action rifle, with a 4/18 scope and *a thick leather sling* in the northwest corner of the TSBD's sixth floor, between some boxes *near the stairway* – just where Lee's spotter had put it. Weitzman and Deputy Sheriff E. L. Boone, both men with above average knowledge of weapons, as well as Deputy Sheriff Roger

Craig and Capt. Will Fritz, identified the make of the rifle, Craig stating that he saw "765 Mauser" stamped into the metal of the rifle. When Capt. Fritz opened its bolt, a live round fell out of the weapon.[127] A 7.65 Mauser shell was recovered in Dealey Plaza.[128]

Then, at 1:37 P.M., on Fort Worth's WBAP radio broadcast: "Crime Lieutenant J. C. Day just came out of that building. Reported British .303 rifle with telescopic lens." By late afternoon, however, the weapon inexplicably had morphed into a 6.5 mm Italian Carcano, which was *supposedly* found on the sixth floor of the TSBD.

A 7.65 Mauser at top, a 6.5 mm Carcano below it.

Supposedly 'Lee Harvey Oswald's' rifle, in the National Archives.

Photo taken by Dallas police of 'Harvey's' rifle.

The Carcano, held by Lt. Day in Police Headquarters. Note the 'sling.'

Although *supposedly* sent from Crescent Firearms to Klein's Sporting Goods in Chicago, that particular Carcano was never shipped to Klein's. 'Harvey's' order was never received by Klein's, because Harvey never sent it – he was at work on March 12, 1963 when the 'order' was supposedly 'mailed.' Klein's had no record of the order. The 'order coupon' furnished to the WC was forged, showing that "A. J. Hidell" had sent it. It obviously didn't have Harvey's fingerprints on it. The coupon was for a 36" rifle – 'Harvey's' rifle was 40" long but the ad was for a 36" Carcano, and at that time Klein's didn't even sell a 40" Carcano rifle.

The Hidell postal money order was never deposited in a bank by Klein's. Harvey's Dallas P.O. box application

179

never listed "Hidell," and the post office wasn't allowed to deliver a weapon to anyone not listed on the form. Harvey couldn't have been given a rifle by the P.O. *without filling out postal form 2162, required to be filled out by <u>both</u> the shipper and the receiver of a firearm.* No such forms were ever found. No Dallas postal worker ever saw the imaginary long package with a rifle in it.[129] By the way, a postal inspector involved in Harvey's case was an FBI informant. He even sat in on one of Harvey's interrogations.[130]

Harvey didn't order a rifle, didn't receive a rifle, didn't take a rifle to New Orleans, didn't bring back to Dallas a rifle from New Orleans – he first went to Mexico City before coming back to Dallas. There was no rifle in Ruth Paine's garage – neither she nor her husband Michael ever saw a rifle. Marina lied to the WC when she said Harvey had a rifle – *no one else ever saw 'Harvey's' rifle.*

Nor did anyone ever see Harvey in the TSBD with a four-foot-long package in brown wrapping paper, or any long package. His fingerprints were not on the rifle, although a palm print taken from his *dead body*[132] was 'found' *days later, supposedly* on a hidden surface of the barrel – <u>after</u> *the FBI reported no finger or palm prints on the rifle.* Never any proof of that palm print – and fingerprint technician Lt. Day told a very fishy story. No fingerprints on the "bag" in which 'Harvey's' rifle was *supposedly* placed. No indications 'his' rifle ever was in the 'bag' that was 'found' in the TSBD – no gun oil nor indentations on the paper.

In WC testimony, experts called the Carcano "a very cheap rifle," "real cheap, common, real flimsy-looking," "a piece of junk," "...very easily knocked out of adjustment." This imported Carcano came from a lot of *defective* rifles which could be bought for $3.00 apiece in lots of 25. It was a manual bolt-action rifle, which could not fire two rounds in 1.7 seconds (the claimed time between the last two heard shots). The rifle had a worn and rusty firing pin.[132] The most expert riflemen called in by the WC were unable to accurately fire three rounds in 5.6 seconds,

The rifle couldn't be sighted by experts because the scope was too wobbly – it had to be repaired before the gun could be test fired. The FBI wrote to the WC that the telescopic sight could not be properly aligned with the target, since the sight reached the limit of its adjustment before reaching accurate alignment. Ammunition for a Carcano would often hang fire – it was last made at the end of World War II. JFK was shot by high velocity rifles – the Carcano was not high velocity – in fact, the Carcano technically wasn't even a rifle—it was a carbine.

And why was that bizarre 'sling' on the Carcano? Where was it obtained, how was it obtained, why was it obtained, how was it to be used? It is just junk. Harvey was a trained U.S. Marine, if not a great shot. Had he purchased a rifle and bullets, he certainly would have bought a real sling if he felt the need for one. And recall that Weitzman said the weapon he found had "a thick leather sling," not a makeshift strap.

More could be said about 'the rifle', but this is enough, especially since *it wasn't Harvey's rifle*. Bottom line: *no one fired that rifle on November 22, 1963*. Years later, Dallas police chief Jesse Curry told newsmen, "We don't have any proof that Oswald fired the rifle and never did. Nobody's yet been able to put him in that building with a gun in his hand."

SHOTS AND CASINGS

Searching the TSBD's sixth floor at 1:00, Deputy Sheriff Luke Mooney found expended shell casings lying on the floor in "a sniper's nest." At 1:12, Lt. Day took a photograph, which appears to show *two empty casings and one round of live ammunition* lying on the floor. Later in the afternoon FBI agent J. Doyle Williams took two photographs of the two empty casings and one round of live ammunition. Five days after the assassination a third empty casing was allegedly received by FBI agent Vincent Drain, allegedly from DPD Captain Will Fritz, who allegedly kept the casing in his possession for five days without telling anyone: Totally unbelievable. The casings and live round were tested for latent fingerprints, with none found.

The House Select Committee on Assassinations (HSCA) later examined the third casing and reported, "Perhaps the most remarkable mark on [the third casing] (CE 543) is a dent in the lip that would prevent it from being fired. The second most remarkable thing is the conspicuous absence of the seating mark found on all the rounds that were known to have come from the rifle...(and) marks indicating loading and extracting at least three times from an unidentifiable weapon...(and) three sets of marks on the base that were not found on any other cartridges that came from [the Carcano]." The HSCA's report has led many critics to conclude that CE 543 was "planted," was never chambered in the Carcano, was added to the evidence by the DPD or the FBI in order to fit the WC's scenario.

Finally, Assassination researcher John Armstrong has written, "WC attorney Joseph Ball was aware the DPD photographs appear to show only two empty shells and handed Luke Mooney a DPD photograph that appears to show two empty cartridges and one round of live ammunition. Ball asked, 'Is that the empty shells you found?' He then handed Mooney a second photograph and said, 'I have another picture. This is a picture taken from another angle. Does that show the cartridges?' [The two photos] are nearly identical, except for one difference. *CE 512* has been altered with the addition of an image that is directly below the live round of ammunition. This image appears to be a crude rendering of an empty casing in both size and shape and appears to be leaning against the brick wall—another doctored photo. If this image was intended to be a casing, then it would be the third empty casing in the photograph, plus the one live round,"[133] No one asked why a live round would be lying on the floor with the casings.

None of this concerned the WC, of course, for in its conclusion it blithely reported three shots, three empty casings. Richard Nixon once told an aide that the assassination cover-up was the greatest hoax ever perpetrated on the American people.

PARKLAND HOSPITAL

Shortly before 1:00, two Catholic priests, Father Oscar Huber and Father James N. Thompson, on their own initiative, had arrived at Parkland and were rushed to

Trauma Room #1, where Father Huber gave JFK the last rites.

At 1:13 Vice President Johnson, waiting in Parkland, was told of JFK's death. Thirteen minutes later, at the insistence of the Secret Service, Johnson left for Love Field. Immediately after his departure, Assistant Press Secretary Malcolm Kilduff announced JFK's death to the waiting world. Johnson arrived at Love Field at 1:33.

~

PLAYGROUND FOR LIARS[134]

The Texas Theatre, November 22, 1963.

There were two sets of falsehoods created around the assassination: one set for JFK, the second for Harvey Oswald, with fantasies jerrybuilt onto reality. Some of

185

those prevarications have already been revealed and discussed. A new group of these came to life soon after 1:00 and played out in the Texas Theatre: its box office, lobby, orchestra, stage, balcony, entrances and exits. The subject of those lies, of course, was Harvey Oswald.

The Texas Theatre is at 231 West Jefferson Boulevard, 1.05 miles from 1026 North Beckley, driving time 2-3 minutes (down Zangs), walking time by a young adult male 18 minutes. So, Harvey couldn't have walked to the Texas Theatre that afternoon – someone drove him, getting him there around 1:08. Who took him there? The two 'policemen' in the black police car? Or? Whatever car it was, Harvey was in it when Tippit was already dead. But why was it so important for Harvey to get to the Texas Theatre – right at that time – that he had to be driven there? Why not walk? Even more to the point, why go to a movie theatre after witnessing the President's murder?

Another time check: how long it would have taken the killer of Tippit to walk from the murder scene to the Texas Theatre. That distance is about .7 of a mile, including the detour to the back of the Texaco gas station and the later return to Jefferson Boulevard. Normal walking time over that distance for a young man would be about 13 minutes. Allowing for Lee's earlier jogging away from the crime scene, lower that to 11 minutes. Lee likely began leaving the crime scene at about 1:08, so adding 11 minutes brings the time of arrival at the theatre to 1:19 at the earliest, *if* Lee didn't stop on the way – which he may have. Now, *if* Tippit *had* been killed at 1:16, as the WC falsely claimed, then Tippit's killer would have reached the theatre around 1:27 P.M., at the earliest, which time is nearly twenty minutes after Harvey arrived there.

The WC said Harvey sneaked into the theatre – not true, *he bought a ticket – 90¢!* What possible motive would he have for sneaking in – he had money in his pocket. Why would he draw attention to himself by sneaking into a theatre at mid-day like a ten-year-old? Remember, he was trained in spycraft by the CIA. He wouldn't do something that stupid.

The theatre's cashier, Julia Postal, was interviewed by researcher Jones Harris in 1963. When asked if she'd sold a ticket to 'Oswald,' Julia burst into tears and left the room. Asked again a little later if she'd sold a ticket to 'Oswald,' she once again burst into tears. Her reactions and refusal to answer this question show that she *did* sell Harvey a ticket. When testifying for the WC, however, she not only said Harvey had "ducked" into the theatre but that "he had a panicked look on his face." Harvey didn't sneak into the theatre. That was a ploy designed by the plotters to draw the police to the theatre.[135]

Twenty-two-year-old Warren 'Butch' Burroughs, who took tickets and ran the theatre's concession stand, *was never asked* by the WC for *any time estimates*. The only 'relevant' thing he *supposedly* told the WC was, "[When the police came.... What did you tell them?] "I said, 'I *haven't seen him* myself. He *might have [sneaked in]*, but *I didn't see him* when he came in. *He must have sneaked in and run on upstairs [to the balcony] before I saw him.*'" "Might have...must have..." – those are not *facts*. Butch wasn't asked and said nothing about selling Harvey popcorn. The WC barely questioned Butch. There was a reason for that.

Butch later told assassination researchers that he knew that "Oswald" had come in "between 1:00 and 1:07," because he had seen him soon after that. Butch also volunteered that he had sold Harvey popcorn at 1:15. Now, would a crazed amateur killer, who in the last forty-five minutes had murdered in cold blood the President of the United States and a Dallas police officer, then had sneaked into a theatre to hide, *come back down* from the balcony and a few minutes later buy popcorn? Then go and sit in the orchestra? In plain sight? And Butch doesn't realize he didn't take a ticket from this man, although there are only about a dozen people in the orchestra, in a theatre seating nine hundred? Does that make any sense?

By now it should be obvious that witnesses were pressured to say what the FBI or WC wanted, that transcripts of testimonies were tampered with, that evidence was altered and manufactured, that some witnesses were terrified. There's also testimony so confusing that it's hard to know what to make of it.

Harvey clearly was in the theatre to meet his intelligence contact, who he apparently did not know. He went into the orchestra and *sat next to* a young man, later identified as Jack Davis, and waited for a prearranged signal. Recall that Harvey had in his pockets a paycheck stub from American Bakeries dated August 22, 1960 – when he was in Russia – and a small white box top with the name "Cox's, Fort Worth." Were these part of a prearranged signal for Harvey's contact, who may have had the bottom of the box, perhaps the cancelled check to match the stub? Why else would Harvey be carrying these? They were trash, otherwise – nothing he'd keep, or carry around with him.

When Jack Davis gave no signal, Harvey got up and sat beside another man across the aisle, waited for the signal,

189

again failed to get it, so he went to the lobby briefly. When he returned, he *sat next to* two more people, the last a pregnant woman, waited twice more, but still no signal. Why not? Because he was supposed to be dead by now – killed either in the TSBD, on the bus or at the bus stop where he'd been expected to get off, or on 10th Street. And consider *why* he would repeatedly sit right next to people in an almost empty theatre if he wasn't looking for a contact.

Before Harvey had come into the theatre there was an event whose time line the WC didn't ask for and the witness didn't volunteer. This witness was twenty-two-year-old Johnny Calvin Brewer, manager of Hardy's Shoe Store, 213 West Jefferson, *nine street numbers* east of the Texas Theatre. His WC testimony somehow doesn't seem quite right – "funny," like the man Johnny said he saw in front of his store.

Aerial view, 231 West Jefferson Avenue (far left), about 230 feet distant from 213, east wall to east wall.

Brewer told the WC on April 2, 1964, that he'd been

listening to a transistor radio about JFK being shot, followed by the news that a police officer had been killed in Oak Cliff. Then he heard a police siren. "I looked up and saw the man enter the lobby [the entryway]...and he stood there with his back to the street....[About how far were you from the front door?] "Ten feet.... I heard the police cars coming up Jefferson, and he stepped in, and the police made a U-turn...at Zangs...and went back down East Jefferson. And when they...left, [the man] looked over his shoulder and turned around and walked up West Jefferson...." How could Johnny tell that the police car made a U-turn at Zangs? He was inside the store, more than twenty feet from the sidewalk, about a hundred feet from the corner of Zangs.

"He was a little man, about 5'9", and weighed about 150 pounds..., brown hair. He had a brown sports shirt on. His shirt tail was out." [Any jacket?] "No." [What color of trousers?] "I don't remember." [Light or dark?] "I don't remember that either." [Any other clothing...?] "He had a T-shirt underneath his shirt." [Was his shirt buttoned up all the way?] "A couple of buttons were unbuttoned at the time." [Why did you happen to watch [him]?] "He just looked funny to me."

This was the first stage of Johnny's ' experience.' There

191

are three problems with this part of his account. First is his immediate belief that he was seeing a dangerous person. Johnny didn't tell the WC he suspected the man had killed Tippit, but in an affidavit, given on *December 2*, 1963, ten days later, Johnny stated that he noticed the man "because he acted so nervous, and I thought at the time he might be the man that had shot the policeman."

The second problem is the time of this event. In his affidavit, Johnny stated, "About *1:30 P.M.* I saw a man *standing* in the lobby of the shoe store." Researcher Joseph McBride has written that the *earliest* commercial radio report of Tippit's shooting was at 1:26 P.M. – so exactly *when did Johnny hear* the report of Tippit's death on his transistor radio? And *what was said*? Four months later, testifying before the WC, there was no mention of the time Johnny saw the "funny" man. In any case, Harvey had been in the Texas Theatre for more than twenty minutes by 1:30.

Third problem was Johnny's description of Harvey's brown shirt and white T-shirt, along with no description of his pants. Remember that *ten days had gone by before his December 2 affidavit.* The man who Johnny *may* have seen in the entryway could have been Lee, who, of course, wasn't wearing a brown shirt – wasn't "a little man." Was Johnny asked by someone to change his description of the man? All that's known is that there wasn't anyone wearing Harvey's brown shirt in the lobby of Johnny's store at 1:30. That shirt was then on Harvey's back in the Texas Theatre. *If* anyone *did* duck into the shoe store lobby at 1:30, and into the Texas Theatre at about 1:34, it was Lee, not Harvey.

And remember that several witnesses at the Tippit murder scene had generally described seeing a white male, dark hair, 160 lbs., 5'10"-5'11" ("Just a nice athletic type...."), dark trousers, *light-colored shirt*, light grayish-tan windbreaker. *Not one mention of a dark rust-brown long-sleeved tweed shirt with the shirt tail hanging out.* That brown shirt contradicts virtually everything the WC said about Harvey prior to his arrest.

Next, the second stage of Johnny Brewer's 'experience'. But first: Johnny had arranged to take this day off from work, and his assistant had agreed to take charge. However, the assistant phoned Brewer to say his newborn baby was ill, and he couldn't come in. So, Brewer came to work that Friday. No assistant in the store.

Continuing: Johnny walked out of his store to the sidewalk (twenty feet), and *watched the "funny" man walk about 230 feet (76.6 yards)*, then "[the man] *walked* into the Texas Theatre, and I walked up to the theatre to the box office – [without hesitation, leaving his store unattended and unlocked?] – and asked Mrs. Postal if she had sold a ticket to a man who was wearing a brown shirt, and *she said no, she hadn't.* She was listening to the radio herself. And I said that a man walked in there, and I was going to go inside and ask the usher if he had seen him."

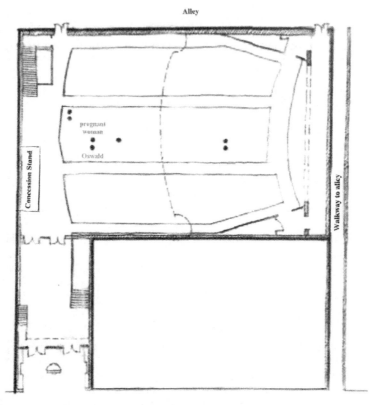

Front entrance of Texas Theatre is at left.

Since it's been deduced that Julia Postal *had* sold Harvey a ticket, it is clear that someone was orchestrating

Julia's and Johnny's testimonies. Witnesses went through their accounts with an FBI agent or WC attorney prior to testifying before the WC, thus there is no way to determine how many accounts came out different in front of the WC – or how many transcripts were altered afterwards.

So, then, the manager of a shoe store, 230 feet east of the Texas Theatre, *supposedly* notices a man in his store's lobby who looks "funny." He comes out of his store to watch – for about 2.5 minutes – this "funny" man *walk* – not trot, not jog, not run, not rush, not dash – *230 feet* west and then *supposedly* "duck" behind the east wall of the theatre entrance. Of course, the "funny" man could have been looking at the movie posters on either side of the ticket booth. Why would Johnny assume immediately that the man had gone into the theatre without paying? And what did Julia Postal mean by "he *ducked* into the theatre," *since she testified she didn't see the man "duck" in*?

Johnny went on: "So I walked in and Butch Burroughs was behind the [concession] counter....and I asked him if he had seen a man in a brown shirt...and he said he...hadn't seen anybody." [Not true!] "And I asked him if he would come with me and show me where the exits were, and we would check the exits. And he asked me why. I told him that I thought the guy looked suspicious.... We walked

195

down to the front of the theatre to the stage. First we checked the front exit, and it hadn't been opened. We went to the back [exit], and it hadn't been opened." Now, actually, Butch *had* to have seen Harvey, since Harvey bought a ticket and went to sit in the orchestra, not the balcony. Lee was sitting in the balcony.

But why even check the exits? Since the concession stand was in the same space as the orchestra seating, if anyone had opened an exit door – it was mid-day – Butch would have seen the light from the alley immediately, and the door did not shut and lock automatically if opened. Didn't it make more sense to first check if the "funny" man had gone up to the balcony, since Butch couldn't see those stairs from his concession stand?

Continuing: "We went back up front and went in the balcony and looked around but we couldn't see anything ...we never did see him. [Yet Lee was up in the balcony!] ...And we came down and went back to the box office and told Julia that we hadn't seen him, and she called the police." If Johnny was so concerned, why didn't he check the men's room too? Great place to hide.

After supposedly *not seeing* the man – in an almost empty theatre, you call the police because a store manager nine doors down the street tells you a man who "looked funny" hadn't paid for a 90¢ theatre ticket? Is that what Julia told the police operator when she supposedly called? And why would Julia agree to call the police anyway? Based on what? She said she *didn't* see Harvey "duck in." And what would Johnny have *done* if he *had* found the man? Johnny must have believed the man was armed and dangerous. His story doesn't pass the smell test.

Meanwhile *Harvey had been in the orchestra the whole time*, sitting three rows down from the back and five seats left into the center section from the right aisle, and Lee had been up in the balcony. Why wouldn't Johnny have seen Harvey? He was in plain sight, brown shirt and all – no one even sitting around him by then – the pregnant woman had left (and was never seen again!). Maybe it was because Johnny had actually seen and was looking for a 'Lee Harvey Oswald' wearing just a white T-shirt, not with a rust-brown tweed shirt over it, i.e., Lee.

Now the third part of Johnny's 'experience': "Butch went to the front exit [of the orchestra], and I went down by the stage to the back exit and stood there...." Hold on – didn't it seem that the "funny" man had gone up to the balcony after "ducking" into the theatre? Now, he and Butch were guarding the fire exits in the orchestra, from where they could not see the front stairs coming down from

197

the balcony, so the "funny" man, having seen two men looking around the balcony, could have gone down the stairs and left the theatre. Not much of a plan.

"Just before [the police] came, they turned the house lights on, and I looked out from the curtains and saw the man." "They" turned the lights on? On a suspicion that a man acting "funny" who hadn't paid for a ticket was in the theatre? Stop the show? Before the police even got there? Why? Weren't "they" afraid this mad murderer would start shooting if "they" tried to apprehend him? And how did Johnny look out from the curtains if he was standing by the exit door, guarding it?

Another time check. At 1:30 Johnny sees the "funny" man stop in the shoe store lobby – for, say, two minutes – who then walks to the theatre, another two minutes, followed by Johnny, another two minutes, so it's at least 1:36 now. Johnny talks with Julia, goes in and talks with Butch, has to be three minutes, all told, so now it's 1:39. They check the exit doors, check the orchestra, go up to the balcony, look around, come down from the balcony, go out and tell Julia to call the police. How long does that take? At least five minutes? OK, 1:44. Julia supposedly calls the cops, while Johnny and Butch go to their fire exits to wait for them, leaving the balcony and theatre front entrances unguarded – anyone could have walked out. But, add one minute more, so 1:45 now. Johnny hears a noise outside, opens his door and sees the alley "filled with police cars." So, Julia called the cops at 1:44, and the cops all got there by 1:45. Believe it or not. Not.

New Orleans District Attorney Jim Garrison later said, "...at least thirty officers [including two captains, two FBI agents, and an assistant District Attorney] in a fleet of patrol cars descend on the movie theatre. This has to be the most remarkable example of police intuition since the Reichstag fire." Several of these policemen (including M. N. McDonald and Gerald L. Hill) came from the Tippit murder scene eight blocks away. How could they get there so fast? And they just left the Tippit investigation?

Johnny Brewer went on: "[Oswald] stood up and walked to the aisle to his right and then turned around and walked back and sat down.... I heard a noise outside, and I opened the door, and the alley...was filled with police cars, and policemen were on the fire exits and around the alley. And they grabbed me, a couple of them, and held and searched me and asked me what I was doing there, and I told them that there was a guy in the theatre that I was suspicious of, and he asked me if he was still there. And I said, yes, I just seen him." [So, we go from "we hadn't seen him" *anywhere* to "call the cops" to "I just seen him" in the orchestra.]

"And he asked me if I would point him out. And I and two or three other officers walked out on the stage, and I pointed him out, and there were officers coming in from the front of the show, I guess, coming toward that way, and officers going from the back."[136]

Imagine what Harvey is thinking. The auditorium lights suddenly come on, but the film is still being projected onto the screen. That smells like trouble, so he gets up and starts to leave, when it strikes him: that's how he'll get killed, "trying to escape." So, he sits back down, and then a couple of cops and some guy come in through a fire exit by the screen, and the guy points in Harvey's direction. More police, with shotguns, enter from the back. Harvey knows the headline, "Assassin attempts escape, is shot dead."

Keep in mind that *Harvey didn't kill Tippit*, wasn't at his murder scene, *didn't even know about Tippit's murder then*. He did think he'd be killed this day, because he must have decided David Atlee Phillips had arranged for the Dallas cops to kill him if he tried to run. So he sat as still as a rock in his seat.

A couple of things need to be cleared up before continuing this account. First, Harvey wasn't driven to the

Texas Theatre just to get there quickly – it was to make certain the "patsy" was where he needed to be. Once he arrived, the one who drove him there either radioed or telephoned that "the target is in place." That was no later than 1:15.

Second, why didn't Lee just go to ground, like every other shooter and associate? *Because he was needed to impersonate Harvey.* Could be no other reason. The plotters needed Lee to enter the theatre, so that Harvey could be killed there in a shootout with police, immediately closing the case. Nothing else makes sense. Otherwise, why was Lee *hurrying* – like at least one witness said – on East 10th Street in the direction of the Texas Theatre? Unless...he was *supposed* to meet and kill Tippit, go to the theatre, and have Tippit's murder blamed on Harvey, as it actually was.

Putting things together:

1. Tippit 'running into' Lee Oswald on 10th Street seems like a *huge* 'coincidence,' especially in light of their Dobbs House encounter two days earlier, as well as Tippit's very strange behavior shortly before encountering Lee.

2. If Lee was only going to the Texas Theatre, why wasn't he just dropped off near the theatre?

3. 'Harvey's' wallet, supposedly 'found' near

201

Tippit, was a plant, meaning it was *planned*.

4. 'Harvey's' pistol, soon to be recovered in the Texas Theatre, was a plant, meaning it was *planned*.

5. If Tippit had *not* been killed, there would have been no reason to plant 'Harvey's' wallet and 'Harvey's' pistol.

6. The police *knew* Harvey was in the Texas Theatre, driven there by police.

7. If Tippit had not been killed, there would have been no cause for a troop of police to come to the theatre.

8. Policemen began arriving at the Texas Theatre at least five minutes before Julia Postal's call, indicating this was *planned*.

9. Considering all this, you have to look very hard at the possibility that Tippit's killing was actually planned and deliberate, to eliminate him for some reason and to incriminate Harvey.

Here's what likely took place: the CIA advised the Dallas police that Harvey would be in the Texas Theatre by 1:30. The "ducking into the theatre without paying for a ticket" ploy was the excuse, the cover story, for a platoon of cops to swoop down on the theatre a few minutes later. Don't ask why Julia and Johnny went along with this fairy tale – just note that witnesses were pressured, witnesses were threatened, witnesses were killed. In any case, this was supposed to be the final, successful, attempt to kill the "lone nut." He was expected to 'resist arrest' and be cut down in the alley by a dozen shotgun-wielding Dallas policemen.

A quick look now at Dallas Police Officer C. F. Bentley Jr. He said he was in the neighborhood and heard a police radio dispatch that a suspect had entered the Texas Theatre and *was in the balcony*. He parked out front, entered the theatre with his shotgun, and was told "by a theatre employee" that the suspect had gone *to the balcony*, so he and another officer quickly went up.

Only three to five people seemed to be there, Bentley reported, but although the house lights were on it was still difficult to see. Just then C. F.'s uncle, Detective Paul Bentley, accompanied by another detective, came up, and Paul told C. F. to search everyone there and take their names. A moment later someone downstairs supposedly yelled, "The son of a bitch is downstairs!" And Paul Bentley and the other three officers ran down the stairs. Why would an officer consider a suspect "a son of a bitch," just because the man failed to buy a 90¢ ticket?

Now, the *official* account of Harvey's arrest: one street

cop, M. N. McDonald, came to Harvey's row of seats and told Harvey to stand up, which he did. Harvey was in the fifth seat in, but McDonald didn't report walking toward him. He told Harvey to raise his hands, which he did, and, McDonald testified, "I put my left hand on his waist and then his hand went to the waist. And this hand struck me between the eyes on the bridge of the nose." [Which fist did he hit you with?] "His *left fist*."

Officer C. T. Walker testified, "McDonald ... was searching, and he felt of his pocket, and Oswald then hit him, it appeared, *with his left hand first, and then with his right hand*." The same right hand that's also pulling out a pistol? So, he had two right hands? He was right-handed.

McDonald *said* Harvey put his right hand on a pistol at his waist, *after* he hit McDonald on his nose – and McDonald put his left hand on Harvey's right hand. Both men fell down between the rows of seats, Harvey on top.

McDonald told a different tale to *The Dallas Morning News*, which two days later quoted him as saying, "A man sitting near the front...tipped me the man I wanted was sitting in the third row from the rear, not in the balcony.... I went up the aisle, and talked to two people sitting about in the middle. I was crouching low and *holding my gun* in case any trouble came." If this was an accurate account,

Harvey would have to have been suicidal to pull a gun on McDonald, who would have been justified to immediately shoot Harvey.

Other cops present in the theatre also testified. Motorcycle officer T. A. Hutson said, "I saw [Officer] McDonald down in the seat beside this person, and this person was in a half-standing crouching position, pushing down on the left side of McDonald's face, and McDonald was trying to push him off." ['This person was right-handed?... He was pushing on the left side of McDonald's face?'] "Right.... And McDonald was trying to hold him off with his hand.... I reached over from the back of the seat with my right arm and put it around this person's throat...and pulled him back up on the back of the seat that he was originally sitting in.

"At this time Officer C. T. Walker came up in the same row of seats where the struggle was taking place and grabbed this person's left hand and held it. McDonald was at this time simultaneously trying to hold this person's right hand. Somehow this person moved his right hand to his waist, and I saw a revolver come out, and McDonald was holding on to it with his right hand, and this gun was waving up toward the back of the seat.... McDonald was using both of his hands to hold onto this person's right

205

hand." What happened to the gun McDonald told the *Morning News* he had in his hand?

Detective Bob Carroll was asked, ['Who had hold of that pistol at that time?'] "I don't know, sir. I just saw the pistol pointing at me, and I grabbed it and jerked it away *from whoever had it*." Now where did Bob Carroll come from? He had been at the TSBD, like Detective Jerry Hill.

So, one cop was holding tight to Harvey's left wrist, another had him pulled back off-balance against the back of his seat in a chokehold, a third cop was grabbing his right wrist, and somehow Harvey *still* reached down to his waist, pulled out a handgun and was waving it toward the back – while the third cop held 'Harvey' gun with his right hand and his right wrist *with both hands* (that makes two right hands on one cop), and a fourth cop pulled the gun from Harvey's right hand. Keep in mind that Harvey weighed a whopping 132 pounds at this time and never worked out. Does this account seem credible? The WC thought so.

Everyone testified they heard the "click" of the trigger of a pistol, but later examination of 'Harvey's' pistol by an FBI technician showed no indentation, no trace, on any bullet, to indicate that the trigger had been pulled and the gun had misfired. Or, perhaps, since *Harvey had no gun*, was that click *McDonald's* pistol, as he tried to kill

Harvey? Except that Harvey grabbed the pistol, so that it couldn't discharge?

Beside Johnny Brewer, only two theatre patrons testified for the WC – although Julia had sold twenty-four tickets. The witness supposedly closest to Harvey was George Jefferson Applin. At the time of Harvey's struggle with McDonald, Applin was standing three rows behind Harvey, in the aisle to Harvey's right. "They came on up to Oswald, where he was sitting.... The officer said, "Will you stand up, please." ...When he stood up, the officer stepped over to search him down.... Oswald – or, the man – took a swing at him. When he did, the officer grabbed him." ['Took a swing at him with his fist?'] "Yes, sir; he did." ['With his left or right?'] *"Right fist...."*

The WC attorney went over the same ground again: ['Then what did Oswald do?'] "He *took a right-hand* swing at him." ['Had you seen the pistol up to that time?'] "No, sir; there was not one in view then." ['How soon after that did you see the pistol?'] "I guess it was about 2 or 3 seconds." ['Who pulled the pistol?'] *"I guess it was Oswald, because – for one reason, that he had on a short-sleeve shirt,* and I seen a man's arm that was connected to the gun." ['...any officers strike him?'] "I seen one strike him with a shotgun.... He grabbed the muzzle of the gun

207

and drawed it back and swung and hit him in the back....with the butt end of the gun." ['...a hard blow?'] "Yes, sir."

Now, three cops were holding Harvey against the back of his seat – how could another one have hit him on his back with the butt of his shotgun? And, of course, Harvey wasn't wearing a short-sleeved shirt – nor holding a pistol. So, although at least seven other young men in the orchestra had a clear view of McDonald and Harvey when things went down, only one other man was called by the WC – and his testimony was even less credible than Applin's. No one was ever able to speak with the rest of those young men, since *the police destroyed the witness list*, probably because nothing claimed by the police actually happened, including the time when Harvey arrived at the theatre.

Accident investigator Ray Hawkins was later asked, "[Did you see anybody strike Oswald during the struggle ...anybody strike him a blow?] "No, sir, I did not see anyone strike him a blow." [Afterwards, did you notice any marks on Oswald's face?] "...Not at that time, but I did notice, however, after I saw him on television that he had a bruise on the right side of his face." [Did you see that bruise there at the theatre?] "Not at the theatre, no, sir." Well, one honest cop.

Harvey twice shouted, "I am not resisting arrest," when he was being taken out. You know why. He also yelled, "I protest this police brutality." Why would he say that if he started the fight?

Why *wasn't* Harvey charged with attempted homicide, if he'd pulled a gun and tried to fire it at a cop in the theatre? Prosecutors always pile on the charges. Why didn't any reporter ask Harvey about drawing a gun? Why *would he* draw a gun? That'd be the best way to get killed. If he drew a gun and tried to fire it, why wasn't he shot? "Drawing a gun on an officer" seems like another part of the "Oswald Legend" – the 'mad killer' part, willing to kill anyone.

Fact is, Harvey never bought a pistol, did not have one in the Texas Theatre. In his article *Oswald Did Not Purchase A Pistol From Seaport* John Armstrong lays out in detail how "A. Hidell" (Harvey's alleged alias) did not order nor pay for nor receive the .38 Smith & Wesson pistol that the WC claimed Harvey used to kill Tippit. For example, several documents required by the Post Office and by Railway Express (which is not allowed to send a firearm to a P.O. box, only to send a notice) before any

209

firearm can be turned over to the purchaser, did not exist for "A. Hidell's" pistol. Ergo, no gun was ever turned over to said (imaginary) person. The pistol allegedly ordered cost $29.95 but "A. Hidell" allegedly was sent a pistol priced at $39.95. The list of facts goes on. There is no way Harvey ordered and received that pistol. To end the matter, the FBI reported that the pistol allegedly taken from Harvey in the Texas Theatre had a bent firing pin and could not have discharged the shots that killed Tippit. So not only wasn't it Harvey's pistol, but it was defective.

So then consider that <u>Harvey never had a pistol</u> with him in the theatre, just as he never had a rifle with him at the TSBD. How could he have the handgun that allegedly killed Officer Tippit if he didn't kill him, wasn't at the murder scene? McDonald claimed that in the Texas Theatre he had his service weapon out. Consider then that he was pointing it at Harvey, was moving toward him, and Harvey – fearing for his life – grabbed McDonald's gun with his left hand, since he expected to be shot, and pushed McDonald backward, falling on him.

Consider a further possibility: that some of the cops already knew Harvey was in the theatre, their instructions were to kill him if he resisted (the platoon in the alley), so he was *protecting himself* from McDonald. The reason the cops didn't shoot Harvey was because there were witnesses present and watching in the orchestra, who would have testified that Harvey didn't draw a pistol, didn't have one. Keep in mind that Harvey was dead when the cops testified – they could say anything they wanted to – and only two witnesses, neither credible, out of those sitting in the orchestra, were ever officially identified or questioned.

How much time had elapsed since the police got to the theatre at 1:45? Let's guess at least six minutes, so 1:51.

The Dallas police arrest report, however, shows the time of Harvey's arrest to be 1:40 (see above), so the Dallas police supposedly arrested Harvey eleven minutes before they actually arrested him and five minutes before they got there. Also note what they accused him of, *with no proof, only an hour and ten minutes after JFK was killed.*

What did the Dallas police *actually* have on Harvey when he was arrested? He was just a man who worked at the TSBD, *who didn't fit Officer Baker's description, who couldn't have been* at 10th and Patton at 1:06 – or even at 1:10, who *wasn't dressed like Tippit's killer and had the wrong build and hair color*, and – if you've been following this tale carefully – *who wore a rust-brown tweed shirt all that day.* Of course, Harvey *supposedly* had a pistol – that *supposedly* killed Tippit – *the one that had a bent firing pin, the one that didn't work, that couldn't shoot, that wasn't Harvey's!* Harvey *supposedly* received 'his' pistol on March 20, 1963, so he *supposedly* would have had it for eight months. Isn't it reasonable to think he would have test fired it at least once and discovered the bent firing pin? Has there ever been a man who bought a rifle or pistol and never test fired it? And how could he have killed Tippit with a pistol like that, had he been there, which he wasn't?

WHAT HAPPENED TO LEE

Before heading for the front doors of the theatre, let's stay inside for a few moments, because, many years later, Butch Burroughs would give some jaw-dropping information to researcher James W. Douglas. Butch said he had seen *a second arrest* in the theatre only three or four minutes after Harvey's. The Dallas police had arrested a young man who "looked almost like Oswald, like he was his brother or something." Butch said he saw both Harvey and this man clearly, and that they looked alike.[137] This is an important identification, because in the space of three or four minutes Butch had seen both of them and could easily compare Lee and Harvey, revealing that Lee actually was not Harvey's "identical twin," just someone with similar features.

Although Harvey was taken out to the *front* of the theatre, Lee was cuffed and taken out a *back* fire exit into the alley. Standing in the alley watching was Bernard J. Haire, owner of Bernie's Hobby House, which was just two doors east of the theatre. He saw police bring out a flushed young white man dressed in slacks and a pullover shirt, put him in a squad car and drive off with him. It wasn't until 1987 that Mr. Haire discovered that the person he'd seen was *not* "Lee Harvey Oswald," not the man Ruby killed.[138]

213

Dallas police files verify Lee's arrest. The official Homicide Report on J. D. Tippit states, "Suspect was later arrested *in the balcony* of the Texas Theatre." In addition, Dallas Police Detective L. D. Stringfellow reported that, "Lee Harvey Oswald was arrested in the balcony of the Texas Theatre." That makes four separate reports about the *second* "Lee Harvey Oswald," Lee Oswald, being in the Texas Theatre.

A short time later, at about 2:00 P.M., T. F. White – a mechanic at Mack Pate's Garage, 114 7th Street, Oak Cliff, just over two blocks southwest of Beckley and Neely, eight blocks north of the Texas Theatre – saw a man he later said he believed was "Lee Harvey Oswald" drive into the parking lot of the El Chico restaurant across the street in a red 1961 Falcon, wearing a white T-shirt. Thinking the man was acting suspiciously, White took down the license plate number of the car, which was "PP 4537." Eventually, word got to the FBI, which checked and found that the license plate actually was issued to a 1957 blue Plymouth which belonged to Carl Amos Mather. That afternoon, Carl had supposedly returned home in his Plymouth at 3:30 P.M.

Mather was employed by Collins Radio, a major contractor with the CIA. During 1963 he had "serviced the communications gear aboard Lyndon Johnson's Air Force

Two," according to researcher Richard Gilbride. Mather was a communications expert, and it's believed there was radio communication between the assassins in Dealey Plaza and the plotters' nearby field headquarters. Someone had to have set up that equipment.

Surprisingly, the FBI sent agents to interview Mather, but he refused to speak with them, citing his high-security clearance. However, his wife Barbara *did* talk with agents, who she told that she and Carl *were close friends of J. D. Tippit and his wife Marie!* KRLD-TV reporter Wesley Wise later interviewed the couple at dinner and reported that, "While the wife was fairly calm, the husband was so upset and agitated that he was unable to eat."[139]

As for what happened next to Lee Oswald on November 22, there's evidence he was flown out of Dallas on an Air Force C-54 the afternoon of the assassination, dropped off at an Air Force base in New Mexico and never seen again.

So the Dallas police department was playing a shell game, just like the CIA plotters: now you see him, now you don't. David Atlee Phillips missed his true calling: he should have been a screenwriter. What is still unknown, though, is how and *why* the second arrest – of Lee Oswald

– came about, and who ordered his release. They'd already arrested "Lee Harvey Oswald" a few minutes earlier.

1:30 P.M.

Bill Shelley was taken *to* police headquarters, charged

Bill Shelley, at right, Danny Arce at left.

with the murder of President Kennedy, held until 5:00 P.M. before being released and required to write a second deposition. No one ever reported why he was arrested or why released.

~

Back at Parkland, journalist Seth Kantor saw Jack Ruby and spoke with him. Another newsman and a woman bystander also saw Ruby there.[140] Why was Ruby at Parkland, especially in light of his activities in the previous eleven hours? For the following forty-six hours, Ruby ran around Dallas, spoke with various persons, and made numerous long distance phone calls to mobsters all over the country, none of which, in the context of the assassination, was ever explained. The WC concluded that Ruby had no mob connections, which, of course, he had had all of his life, nor had run guns to Cuba for the CIA, which he unquestionably had.

~

Secret Service agent Clint Hill had ordered a casket for President Kennedy's body, and it had arrived at 1:30.[141] By 1:40 the body was in the casket, wrapped in a sheet, ready to depart for Air Force One. Or so the Kennedy entourage and Clint Hill thought. Just arrived Dallas County Coroner Earl Rose had a different thought.

~

Darrell C. Tomlinson, Parkland's senior engineer, removed a stretcher from an elevator and placed it in the corridor on the ground floor, alongside another stretcher. Gov. Connally had been on one of these stretchers. A few minutes later, he bumped one of the stretchers against the wall and a bullet dropped to the floor. Although Tomlinson was not certain whether the bullet came from Gov. Connally's stretcher or the adjacent stretcher, the WC concluded that the bullet came from Connally's stretcher, having fallen out of Connally's left thigh – despite other bullet fragments still in his thigh, despite having gone through both Connally's body and JFK's body, despite

217

having shattered Connally's right fifth rib and right wrist (and left bullet fragments in it) and despite being in almost pristine condition. So was born the legend of the "magic bullet," supposedly fired by Lee Harvey Oswald.

~

1:40 P.M.

Coroner Earl Rose was insisting that JFK's body had to be autopsied in Dallas, but Secret Service agent Clint Hill and the Kennedy aides were equally adamant that the body leave for Washington, D.C. immediately. After a violent verbal confrontation, the summoning of a Justice of the Peace, and District Attorney Wade's phoned agreement to let the body be moved, the agents pushed Rose and the J.P. "against the wall at gunpoint and swept out of the hospital with the President's body."[142] The casket was placed in a hearse and, along with Mrs. Kennedy and others, the hearse and escort roared off for Love Field at 2:08.

~

As all this was taking place, Lyndon Johnson, aboard Air Force One, was insisting he must be sworn in as President *in Dallas* by Federal Judge Sarah Hughes and that Jacqueline Kennedy had to be present for the swearing in. After a frantic search, Judge Hughes was located and asked to come to Air Force One.

1:50 P.M.

Having overpowered Harvey, the police brought him outside. There was a virtual lynch mob before the theatre. Harvey was shoved into a police car, a detective sitting on either side of him. As they fled from the bloodthirsty crowd and drove toward police headquarters, another 'legend' came into being. The story was that *supposedly* Detective Paul Bentley, sitting next to Harvey's left, asked him his name, and when Harvey didn't answer, Bentley took Harvey's wallet from a pants pocket, looked through the wallet and supposedly found two IDs, one for "Lee Harvey Oswald," the other – a Selective Service card – for "Alek J. Hidell."

There were problems with this account, researcher Sylvia Meagher later pointed out.[143] The first and biggest was that no one at all – no policemen, no detectives, not the lead detective, not the chief of police, not an assistant D.A., not the D.A., not the FBI, not the Secret Service – ever spoke of "Alek J. Hidell " on this Friday. Mentioned was "O. H. Lee" and, of course, "Lee Harvey Oswald," but no "Alek J. Hidell." That's because the police didn't receive

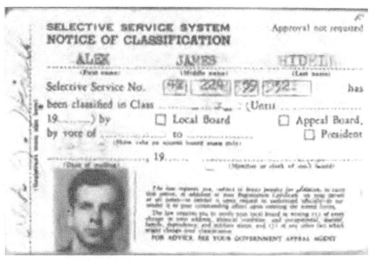

This photograph has the right half of Lee's face, the left half of Harvey's, and it's not Harvey's chin.

the Hidell ID until Saturday, Ms. Meagher believed. And the *supposed* "Alek J. Hidell" ID at the Tippit murder scene? You'd think they would have shouted that to the rooftops! But no – silence covered it, like the cloak of night.

Selective Service cards didn't have photographs on them. So, why did this bogus one have one? To make it easy to identify Harvey quickly. And where did that old photo with half Lee's face and half Harvey's face come from? The CIA. The card was made by the CIA, or FBI or Chauncey Holt. One more anomaly: the WC noted that "the arresting officers found a forged selective service card with a picture of Oswald and the name 'Alek J. Hidell' in Oswald's billfold." The ID *supposedly* found in Harvey's arrest wallet, as you can see above, reads "Alek *James* Hidell," so could there have been two *different* ID cards? When Harvey was arrested in New Orleans on August 9, 1963, no Selective Service "Hidell" card was found in his wallet, although he was assumed to have forged the card at work in Dallas before leaving for New Orleans.

The card appeared on Saturday in order to tie Harvey to the forged order form for the Carcano rifle, which would tie him to the rifle, which *supposedly* would tie him to the murder of President Kennedy. All of it trying to frame Harvey.[144] Yet at that time in Texas he could have bought a rifle across the counter with *no* ID, and no one would have known he'd bought it. So, why would he order a rifle by mail using a false name?

The Hidell name actually had a history, but it was not being used as an alias. On June 3, 1963 Harvey opened a New Orleans P.O. box, supposedly listing a second name,

"A. J. Hidell," but that actually was a forgery, written on his postal application after Harvey's death by Marina. Hidell was a name *given to Harvey by the CIA after he went to New Orleans,* and it was used not only by him but also by other intelligence operatives. *It was not an alias –* he never used the name as an alternate identity, for anything. *"Hidell" was a project code name –* and it never was on Harvey's previous P.O. box application in Dallas either, because back then he hadn't been given that code name yet. He also used "Alek James Hidell." In Russia people had called him "Alek." Different configurations of the name were for different code purposes.

One of those using the code name "Hidell," *and* the variant "Hidel" (along with different first and middle names), was CIA contract agent Richard Case Nagell, who actually had created the "Hidell" name, researcher Dick Russell has written in *The Man Who Knew Too Much.*

Ten years after the assassination, ex-CIA agent and assassination researcher George O'Toole came across a newly (1973) invented investigative tool: Voice Stress Analysis (VSA), which could measure degrees of vocal stress caused by degrees of lying.[145] The beauty of the technique is that the subject is not present for the analysis. Audio tapes – past or present – of the subject are fed into a

222

device, the Psychological Stress Evaluator (PSE).[146]

Intrigued, O'Toole bought a PSE device and was trained to operate it. The degrees of stress using PSE were classified as "no stress," "moderate stress," "good stress," and "hard stress." So, "hard stress" is a barefaced lie. One of the first things to catch O'Toole's attention was 'Harvey's' Alek J. Hidell ID card.

Detective Paul Bentley, center, taking Harvey from the Texas Theatre, Sgt. Jerry Hill behind Bentley.

O'Toole soon became interested in Detective Paul L. Bentley, who helped in arresting Harvey and who sat to his left in the police car as Harvey was taken to police headquarters. O'Toole (O) interviewed and audio taped Bentley (B) in 1973 and analyzed his statements with PSE:

B. [Oswald's] gun was in his right hand.

Good to hard stress shown.

O. Which pocket was his wallet in?

223

B. Left rear pocket.

Hard stress shown.

O. ...he had both Hidell and Lee Harvey Oswald [IDs]?

B. There was three or four different names...in there.

Hard stress shown.

In a police report Bentley filed on December 3, 1963, he made only one reference to the wallet: "On the way to City Hall I removed the suspect's wallet and obtained his name." But even that is doubtful now. When asked on TV if he was "familiar with this subject [Oswald]:"

B. No, I'd never seen him before.

Hardest stress shown.

Julia Postal later said that when Harvey was taken out of the theatre, officers arresting him identified Harvey to her by name – Lee Harvey Oswald – and her statement is in the WC files.

Bentley's responses indicate that Harvey had no handgun, that Bentley did not take Harvey's wallet from his pocket to check on Harvey's name, and that there was no Hidell card. And where had Bentley seen Harvey before? At a meeting of conspirators that Harvey had attended?

O'Toole also interviewed Police Sergeant Gerald "Jerry" L. Hill, who not only was present when 'Harvey's' rifle shells were 'found' in the TSBD, but who also showed up at the Tippit murder scene and was present when 'Harvey's' vanishing wallet was 'found,' was at the Texas Theatre and handled 'Harvey's' pistol, finally was in the police car with Harvey and was party to the Hidell ID episode – present when almost every piece of false 'evidence' against Harvey was 'found.' Then Hill was interviewed on radio to talk about these 'finds.' Does all this arouse anyone's curiosity?

O'Toole noticed that although Hill told him that Harvey's wallet had contained the Hidell card, Hill had made no mention of the Hidell name during a detailed radio interview he gave on the afternoon of November 22. Like Sylvia Meagher, O'Toole questioned Hill's omission.

O'Toole fed a few of Hill's taped comments into his PSE device and later wrote that,

> A statement by Hill that 'We took his billfold out of his pocket' begins with virtually no stress but reaches good stress on the word 'pocket.' Stress reaches good to hard level during, 'we found the ID in both names, Oswald and Hidell,' and [good to hard level stress] remains there during, 'He had library cards and draft cards in one name, and he had identification cards from various organizations

in the other name.' O'Toole also found *hard stress* on a tape of a CBS interview with Hill about the shells from the Carcano rifle 'found' at the TSBD.

Why were Bentley and Hill stressed about removing Harvey's wallet and cards from a back pocket, and why didn't Hill mention the Hidell card Friday? Simple. The police didn't get the Hidell card from the CIA/FBI until Saturday, and they'd said nothing about it on Friday – because the CIA/FBI had told them nothing about "Hidell" on Friday – so the police had to account for how they got their hands on the Hidell card. Like screenwriters, they had to create a "back story" to explain where the card had come from.

Someone made up the tale of Harvey refusing to give his name in the car and Bentley *supposedly* reaching for Harvey's wallet and *supposedly* finding the Hidell card, along with Harvey's other cards. In reality, however, Harvey's wallet never left his pocket before he was booked – because Bentley and Hill already knew his name – and there was no "Hidell" card in his wallet.

Most likely the favored scenario of the plotters had been that the assassination was carried out by Cuban shooters sent by Fidel Castro, but – probably as late as

226

Friday afternoon – the highest level of the cabal vetoed that story, believing it too dangerous. The fallback legend was the "lone nut," but the materials for this weren't made available to the Dallas police on Friday. After planning the ambush for more than a year, it's hard to understand why so many mistakes were made about 'Lee Harvey Oswald' *if* he'd been the chosen patsy all along.

A couple of things to finish the subject of 'Harvey's' names: First, at 3:15 P.M. this day, the 112th Army Military Intelligence Group *supposedly* notified *the FBI* that Harvey was using the name "Hidell." This, apparently, was *supposedly* after the Dallas police had called Lt. Colonel Robert Jones "advising that an A. J. Hidell" had been arrested in Dallas. Remember that Harvey did not get to police headquarters until shortly after 2:00. Who called Jones and when and why?

Jones was an operations officer, and he *supposedly* quickly located the "Hidell" file, which was cross-referenced with another file on "Oswald." So, what was in the "Hidell" file – *if it ever existed?* No one knows. *Supposedly*, the WC never requested the file, and *supposedly* the file was 'routinely' destroyed by the Pentagon in 1973.

Second, on the day of the assassination Harvey was

"mistakenly" identified as "Harvey Lee Oswald" by the Dallas police and Army Intelligence. That name, reported assassination researcher Peter Dale Scott, was found more than two dozen times – starting in June, 1960 – in the files of the FBI, CIA, ONI, Secret Service, Dallas Police, Army Intelligence, and the Mexican Secret Police (DFS). So, obviously, no clerical error.

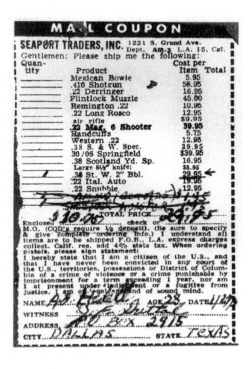

Then there's the matter of 'Harvey's' pistol, supposedly taken from him in the Texas Theatre, that the WC claimed also was ordered by mail on January 27, 1963, by "A. J. Hidell," with another bogus order coupon from some magazine (above. Harvey's fingerprints were not on the coupon, of course. As with the Carcano, the pistol 'ordered' was different from the pistol 'sent.'

2:10 P.M.

BOOKED & QUESTIONED

As Harvey was taken into police headquarters, a detective asked him if he wanted his head covered. "Why should I hide my face," Harvey replied, "I haven't done anything to be ashamed of."[147] During the booking process Harvey had to empty his pockets, and – it was later reported – he *supposedly* had five loose pistol rounds in his pants pockets. However, a Dallas Police Property Clerk Receipt [148] and an FBI report[149] do not list any bullets in Harvey's pockets.

Harvey was then brought to an interrogation room upstairs. "[Oswald] seemed quite calm, much calmer than I would have been," a detective later said. He asked Harvey about shooting Tippit, and Harvey responded, "I didn't shoot anybody!"

When Detective Captain Will Fritz learned who Harvey was, Harvey was moved to Fritz's office, and Fritz started questioning him at 2:25. Eventually Fritz asked Harvey if he had shot the president, and Harvey told him, "No. I emphatically deny that." Then Fritz asked if Harvey had shot Tippit. "No. I deny that, too," Harvey replied. He also was asked by an FBI agent if he'd been to Mexico City, which surprised Harvey. How did a local FBI agent know about Harvey being in Mexico City? A "lone nut"? Obviously, the FBI agent was referring to the false tale told by the CIA, which Harvey knew nothing about, while Harvey thought the agent was asking about Harvey's actual trip to Mexico City. This was the type of confusion that the CIA rogues worked diligently to create.

Fritz asked where Harvey was when the President was shot, to which Harvey replied, "Outside with Bill Shelley." Saying that caused the FBI to immediately get hold of the Altgens6 photo and remove Bill Shelley from beside Harvey, and then everyone claimed that Harvey's figure was Billy Lovelady.

So began the governmental cover up of the Kennedy assassination, which has lasted to this day.

2:20 P.M.

AIR FORCE ONE

The hearse arrived, JFK's casket was taken aboard Air Force One; Jackie, Clint Hill and the others boarded the plane. Not long after, Judge Sarah Hughes arrived, and at 2:38 Lyndon Johnson was sworn in as the 36th President of the United States. At 2:47 Air Force One took off for Washington, D.C.[150]

4:30 P.M.

POLICE HEADQUARTERS

Harvey was taken for his first lineup. The lineups were all rigged. For example, Harvey always was photographed wearing just a T-shirt and dark pants. What happened to the rust-brown tweed shirt he wore when arrested? After he was brought to police headquarters he was never again seen with that shirt on. The reason? The killer of J. D. Tippit was described as wearing dark pants and a light shirt under a jacket. No mention ever of a rust-brown tweed shirt that was hanging out. So the police couldn't put Harvey in a lineup wearing a rust-brown shirt.

And the three men in the first lineup with Harvey not only didn't look at all like him (they were larger and taller) but two had suits and ties and, of course, they didn't have bruises on their faces. Harvey protested: "You are trying to railroad me…. You are doing me an injustice by putting me out there dressed different than these other men…. I am…the only one with a bruise on his head…. I don't believe the lineup is fair, and I desire to put on a jacket similar to those worn by some of the other individuals in the lineup. All of you have a shirt on, and I have a T-shirt on. I want a shirt or something…. This T-shirt is unfair."

Harvey was returned to Fritz's office at 4:45, and Fritz began questioning Harvey again. He told Fritz. "I want to talk with Mr. Abt, a New York attorney…. I have not been given the opportunity to have counsel…." Then, dejectedly, "Everybody will know who I am now," meaning that his intelligence work would be revealed.

Taken to his second lineup at 6:30, he shouted to reporters in the hall, "I didn't shoot anyone…. I never killed anybody." Later in the day they put three teenagers in another lineup with him. He protested again, "It isn't right to put me in line with these teenagers." They also brought in witnesses who had already seen Harvey on television. Even then, a lot of witnesses couldn't identify him without nudging by the police. It was all a sham.

Harvey was arraigned for the murder of Officer Tippit at 7:10. In the hall again at 7:50, he yelled, "I am only a patsy." Questioning was continued in Fritz's office at 8:00 by an FBI agent, but Harvey had had enough, "I believe I've answered all the questions. I don't care to say anything else."

~

At Bethesda Naval Hospital in Maryland, the autopsy

of President Kennedy's body began in the evening. An extensive account of this was chronicled by David Lifton in his book *Best Evidence*. A summary of his findings is presented in the *Appendix* of the present book.

~

Just before 9:00 P.M., Harvey was fingerprinted and given a paraffin test on his hands and cheek. He told the detectives, "What are you trying to prove with this paraffin test, that I fired a gun? You are wasting your time. I don't know anything about what you are accusing me." They found no gunpowder residue on Harvey's cheek or hands, and although nitrates were found or his hands, nitrates are found in ink, which was on boxes he'd handled for four hours that morning.

Harvey tried to make a long distance phone call shortly before 10:45 P.M. but was told it didn't go through, which was a lie. Here's what happened: the two police phone operators on duty – Alveeta Treon and Louise Swinney – were told that two lawmen would soon come to listen in on a call Harvey would be making. The men arrived, showed their credentials, and went into a room next to the switchboard. Around 10:45 a red light blinked on the telephone panel, showing Harvey had picked up the handset in the jail phone booth.

233

Swinney alerted the two agents and handled the call, as Treon listened in on line and wrote down on a message slip what Harvey said. He asked to call a "John Hurt" collect, and gave Swinney two North Carolina numbers. She wrote these down and began to put the call through to the first number. "I was dumbfounded at what happened next," Mrs. Treon later said. "Mrs. Swinney opened the key to Oswald and told him, 'I'm sorry, the number doesn't answer.' She then unplugged and disconnected Oswald without ever trying to put the call through. A few moments later Mrs. Swinney tore the page off her notation pad and threw it into the wastepaper basket."

Treon kept the slip with the notes she had written on it as a souvenir.[150] Researchers later found that the numbers were for two Raleigh men – John D. Hurt and John W. Hurt – both of whom denied knowing about "Lee Harvey Oswald" and his attempted phone call, but one of the men, John David Hurt, served in U.S. military counter intelligence during World War II.[151] And one thing that has been learned about intelligence services is that there's no such thing as a 'former' intelligence officer.

Some researchers feel that John David Hurt may have been a military intelligence "cutout," someone who would pass on an agent's seemingly innocuous message to an

234

intelligence handler, without the "cutout" knowing who the agent was or what the agent might be involved in, insulating the "cutout" from any criminal act and creating space between the agent and his handler, allowing for "plausible deniability."

What no one seems to have questioned over all these years is why Harvey had memorized the phone numbers of these two Raleigh, North Carolina men. But the call was a mistake on Harvey's part – an intelligence operative later told a researcher that Harvey would have been killed for just attempting the call, since that was a lead that could have exposed the entire plot eventually if it had been properly investigated. Neither the WC nor the HSCA looked into this event.

~

The cover-up went spinning along later this day. District Attorney Henry Wade had told reporters that "preliminary reports indicated that more than one person was involved in the shooting." However, Cliff Carter, Lyndon Johnson's aide, phoned Wade "three times this evening from the White House.... He said that President Johnson felt any word of a conspiracy...would shake our nation to its foundation."[152] Wade stopped talking about a conspiracy.

235

~

Harvey was supposedly arraigned at 11:26 P.M. for the murder of President Kennedy,[153] then taken to a news conference. A newsman asked, "Did you kill the President?" Harvey told him, "No.... I did not do it. I did not do it – I did not shoot anyone." Jack Ruby was in the back of the room, and, he later said, had his pistol in a pocket.

9:00 P.M.

AN ODD ARREST

The day should have concluded with Harvey's news conference, but it didn't. Earlier, at 6:45, Wesley Frazier had been arrested, the Randle home searched, and a .303 caliber British rifle with ammunition belonging to Frazier confiscated. *Why* this happened is still a mystery.

However, that wasn't the end of the incident, for as Frazier was being taken back to his home in Irving at 9:00, the police driving him were radioed to return him to police headquarters, where Captain Fritz asked Frazier to take a lie detector test. That supposedly ended at 12:10 A.M., and Frazier *supposedly* passed it with flying colors. Routine, unimportant, one might say.

It was anything but routine, for ten years later George O'Toole became very interested in Frazier and began by analyzing a CBS recording of Frazier telling his "Oswald curtain rods" story:

"PSE analysis of this [CBS] recording revealed a remarkable degree of stress throughout. It was such a classic example of the smooth, maximum hard stress waveform, maintained through almost the entire statement, that a PSE specialist to whom I showed it remarked, 'On a scale of ten, this stress is somewhere near eleven.' ...When Frazier made his statement, he was in a condition of sheer terror," O'Toole later wrote in his book.

O'Toole spoke with Dallas detectives once more. When he asked Paul Bentley – senior polygraph examiner for the Dallas police – about Frazier's polygraph exam, Bentley replied, "I don't recall that even occurring," which statement brought forth *maximum hard stress*. When Detective R. D. Lewis was asked if he'd tested Frazier, he said, "No, I don't remember giving anybody one," eliciting *hard stress*. Isn't that interesting– two veteran Dallas police polygraph experts nailed by VSA ten years later.

When Jerry Hill told O'Toole that Captain Fritz didn't believe in polygraphs, so didn't use them, *near-maximum stress* appeared. Detective Richard Stovall vaguely recalled a Frazier exam, but when asked if only Frazier and the examiner were present replied, "Well, as far as I know," eliciting *hard stress*. Detective Guy Rose said, "There was only one officer in the room with him" and "[Frazier] was telling just exactly the truth," which statement resulted in *hard stress*. Why were *five detectives* lying about the polygraph exam? Jim Bishop wrote that there were five police officers *in the room* during the polygraph exam and that Frazier's responses "bordered on controlled hysteria."

In 1973 O'Toole found a man – formerly with both the FBI and the CIA – to locate Frazier, but the man's FBI contact emphatically refused any information – Frazier's file was "red tagged," which meant the FBI was still keeping an eye on him *ten years later*. Why, if he was just an ordinary witness? But O'Toole finally got lucky, hiring private investigator Anthony Pellicano, who found Wesley Frazier (F) in forty-eight hours and taped a phone interview with him, which both O'Toole and Pellicano analyzed, separately, with PSE. Here are the highlights of Frazier's statements, with results:

F. "Lee" wanted to go get curtain rods Thursday afternoon:
Maximum hard stress.

F. More about "Lee" and the curtain rods:
Nearly maximum hard stress.

F. Said "Lee" took the package into the TSBD:
Maximum hard stress.

F. Only the polygraph operator was in the room with Frazier:

Maximum hard stress.

F. Frazier passed the polygraph test and did well:

Maximum hard stress.

F. He didn't know who Paul Bentley was:

Maximum hard stress.

Forty years later journalist Markus Schmidt interviewed Frazier and wrote:

"Police arrested Frazier as a suspected accomplice of Oswald's.... He was fingerprinted, photographed and forced to take a lie detector test. 'I was interrogated and questioned for many, many hours,' Frazier said. 'Interrogators would rotate.' Dallas police Capt. Will Fritz, who was in charge of the homicide department, came into the room with a typed statement. He handed Frazier a pen and demanded he sign it. It was a confession. Frazier refused. 'Captain Fritz got very red-faced, and he put up his hand to hit me, and I put my arm up to block. I told him we'd have a hell of a fight, and I would get some good licks in on him. Then he stormed out the door.' ...At around 3:00 A.M. the next day, police let Frazier go."[154]

So, what was this all about? Have to conclude Wesley was threatened to spin the story he later did or be accused of being Harvey's accomplice.

Saturday, November 23

10:30 A.M.

Harvey was again interrogated in Capt. Fritz's office, where he told Fritz, "I am familiar with all types of questioning and have no intention of making any statements.... I didn't tell Wesley Frazier anything about bringing back some curtain rods.... I did carry a package to the Texas School Book Depository – I carried my lunch, a cheese sandwich and fruit, which I made at Paine's house." Recall that, supposedly, there was no stenographer present, nor was a tape recorder used, at any of Harvey's interrogations, so these statements are what others said they recalled or wrote in notes. Yet notice the stiff and foreign-sounding language so typical of Harvey.

1:15 P.M.

Harvey spoke with Marina and his bogus 'mother,' and at 2:15 another rigged lineup was held with him, again in his T-shirt. At 3:30 his 'brother' Robert came. Robert was in a quandary. He was the brother of the real Lee Oswald,

241

son of the real Marguerite Oswald, and also had actually lived for a year with Harvey and his 'mother'.

But now he had a problem: he'd only signed up to help a CIA agent – 'Harvey' – but had become an inadvertent party to an assassination. Of course, he had no idea if Harvey was involved or not – Robert hadn't seen Harvey for a year. Harvey told Robert, "I don't know what is going on. I just don't know what they are talking about.... Don't believe all the so-called evidence." When Robert looked into Harvey's eyes for a clue, Harvey said to him, "Brother, you won't find anything there." Addressing Robert as "brother," rather than "Robert" or "Bob" again sounds more foreign than American.

~

Time unknown

Capt. Fritz later told a researcher that sometime during this Saturday Lyndon Johnson called him and said, "You've got your man, the investigation is over."[1]

6:25 P.M.

BACKYARD PHOTO

Harvey was once more talking with Fritz, who showed Harvey the "backyard" photograph, in which 'Harvey' was holding 'his' pistol, 'his' rifle, and copies of *The Militant* and *The Worker* in the backyard of 212-214 W. Neely

Street. This photo was bogus from start to finish. Harvey told Fritz as much: the photo was fake, a forgery. Harvey knew because he had worked in a photo lab for seven months during the previous year.

First, there was something wrong with the head – it seemed to be more in focus than the rest of the picture, too big for the body under it, and not set right on the neck. Then, the shadows on the face go straight down, but the shadow behind the figure angles to the right. And it's obvious that the chin isn't Harvey's – it's square, not pointed, with no cleft – and you can see where Harvey's face is attached at the chin. Then, the right arm and hand

Harvey's chin.   *Not Harvey's chin!*

belong to a man larger than Harvey – plus the tips of the fingers seem to be missing.

Harvey told Fritz that the upper part of his face had been glued onto the picture, and he'd be able to prove that. Three different versions of the photograph eventually surfaced, and researchers later showed other things wrong with the picture. Police photographer Roscoe White was suspected of helping to fabricate the photo, possibly posing for it.

Last, but not least, was the Imperial Reflex camera *supposedly* used by Marina to take the backyard photos. It wasn't among Harvey's things at his rooming house; it wasn't found at Ruth Paine's house; and Marina first described a very different camera she said she used to take the photos. 'Harvey's' Imperial Reflex camera first surfaced *three months* after November 22, on February 14, 1964 *when 'brother' Robert gave it to the FBI*. So, where did Robert – who lived in Fort Worth – get the camera? *Supposedly* from Ruth Paine, who lived in Irving and repeatedly came up with evidence to frame Harvey in the months after the assassination, long after the police had gone over her house and garage with a fine-tooth comb.

NEELY STREET

Here's what this was all about: the CIA/FBI wanted to incriminate Harvey with the "backyard" photo. For that, they needed a backyard for the picture, one that was somewhat secluded. Harvey's previous residence, the Elsbeth Apartments had no such back yard, but 212-214 W. Neely Street, apparently another CIA "safe house," did have a suitable yard.

The WC claimed that Harvey, Marina and June had lived upstairs and that another couple had lived downstairs. Notice that there's no house next door at the left, nor does there seem to be one at the right, so no nosy neighbors. The back yard also seems to be secluded, perfect for shooting

245

the bogus "backyard photo." A 1963 document notes that "there are no other houses facing on Neely Street in the

212-214 W. Neely Street.

212-214 back yard.

246

block where this residence is located." So, this structure was somewhat isolated, ideal for a CIA "safe house."

The only 'evidence' to 'prove' that Harvey lived at 214 W. Neely for seven weeks is an affidavit dated *June 12, 1964*, in which an M. Waldo George, claiming to be office manager of the Tucker Manning Insurance Company of Dallas, stated that he owned the Neely Street duplex and rented the upper floor to Harvey on March 2, 1963.

Problems with the affidavit: 1) there were no rent receipts or any other records, 2) the FBI submitted no utility or phone bills for that address, 3) Waldo George also was listed in WC documents under the names F. M. George and Jim W. George, 4) no researcher is known to have found and interviewed George, 5) 202 days went by before George's sworn affidavit supposedly was taken, and 6) residents on the block had never seen Harvey and his family.

George and his wife didn't testify for the WC. Why? The Elsbeth Apartments managers, Mahlon Tobias and his wife, *did* testify, on April 2, 1964.[2] Landlady Mary Bledsoe testified, on April 2, as did housekeeper Earlene Roberts, on April 8, and even Dallas YMCA desk clerk Colin Barnhorst, on April 1, along with Harvey's New Orleans landlady, Jesse Garner, on April 6. The Georges were the only Dallas landlords not called to testify, and Waldo's affidavit was taken in June, rather than early April, when all the others testified.

Waldo George also stated in the affidavit that the downstairs unit was occupied by Mr. and Mrs. George B. Gray, who were never interviewed by the FBI and who have never been found by researchers. George stated on November 29, 1963, that the Grays occupied 212 W. Neely from February 16 to May 1 but that he "believed they had left Dallas…and he had no idea how to locate [them]." To add insult to injury, George said that the Grays had *supposedly* called him to complain that "the man in the upstairs apartment was beating his wife." But did the Grays even have a phone? They weren't listed in the 1963 Dallas telephone directory. And when Marina was asked by the WC if there was "any violence or any hitting of you? Did that occur on Neely Street?" Marina replied, "No, that was on Elsbeth Street." This *supposed* 'report' by the Grays was part of Harvey's demonization – 'the vicious husband.'

The supposed existence of the Grays is anchored completely in M. Waldo George's affidavit and other statements. The Dallas City Directory of 1963 listed the 214 W. Neely Street apartment as vacant in 1962 and Lillie Hoover (supposedly the owner of the property that year but never found by researchers) as living in the downstairs apartment at 212 W. Neely. The 1964 Dallas City Directory listed both Neely apartments as empty in 1963.

So, nothing is known about Mr. and Mrs. George B. Gray – or even that there ever *was* a George B. Gray, and there's nothing to show that M. Waldo George's affidavit has any truth to it.

In another statement, on November 29, George said "he was in error" that the Oswalds had resided at 214 W. Neely Street from April 1 to May 31, 1963, now saying the dates were from March 2 to May 1. That change was needed by the WC because Harvey left Dallas for New Orleans on April 25. However, Mr. and Mrs. Marvin Friddle, 702 N. Madison Ave., on November 29, 1963 told the FBI they didn't know the Oswalds but "do know that a young man, his wife, and *two small children* had resided at the upstairs apartment [214 Neely]...for a very short time, around April and May – they would see him, his wife and *children* around the house and on the upstairs balcony." Obviously not the Oswalds.

So, the bogus "backyard" photo was embedded in the 'legend' that the Oswald family had lived on Neely Street for seven weeks in 1963. That should have ended the legend of the 'murderous commie' who killed JFK, but the

CIA wouldn't let it go at that. They wanted to depict Harvey as a monster – because only a mentally deranged monster would kill a president.

THE FANTASY

Consequently, the CIA decided to paint a phantasmagorical background around the figure of 'Lee Harvey Oswald' worthy of Hieronymous Bosch. As their chief painter they chose Marina Oswald, a dubious and inept artist, and instructed her to depict the following scene:

In late January, Harvey supposedly filled out a form to purchase a mail-order revolver, and the coupon was supposedly received by Seaport Traders on March 13. At the beginning of March, Harvey supposedly was asked to leave his Elspeth apartment because other tenants supposedly had complained that Harvey was drinking, yelling and beating Marina. Supposedly, the Oswalds immediately moved to West Neely Street on March 3. The next weekend, March 9-10, Harvey supposedly reconnoitered the home of former U. S. General Edwin Walker, 4011 Turtle Creek Blvd, Dallas (6.6 miles north of Neely Street, reached by a complex route), and photographed his house – the picture later 'found' in Ruth Paine's magical garage, which on command could crank out any needed 'evidence' against Harvey. Not known is when and where the film was developed, and what and where the other pictures on the roll were.

On March 12, Harvey supposedly mail-ordered a Carcano rifle, and on March 25 he supposedly went to the downtown post office after work and picked up a 40" rifle – though the order was for a 36" rifle. He supposedly went home on a bus, but no one saw him with the package. He got off the bus, but no one saw him walk to his residence. Marina did not see the package when Harvey got home, nor did she see him unwrap the rifle, nor see the box or packing material it had been shipped in. Harvey made no complaint to the seller about getting the wrong rifle.

In the same time frame, Harvey 'received' the wrong revolver – he had ordered a $29.95 revolver but supposedly was sent, by American Express, addressed to his P.O. box, a $39.95 revolver instead.

On March 31 – a cloudy and rainy day – Marina supposedly photographed 'Harvey' in a sunny Neely Street back yard, proudly holding the rifle and two newspapers, the revolver in a holster on 'his' hip, like a kid who got a cap pistol and a BB rifle for Christmas. No one knows where 'his' holster came from, or when. Marina said she took the pictures "towards the end of February, possibly the beginning of March" – although Harvey supposedly got the guns on March 25.

On April 10, Harvey supposedly came home, ate dinner, then took the rifle out of the house, without Marina seeing him, walked down the street to a bus stop, rode one or more busses to General Walker's neighborhood, set up his shot without being seen, fired one round into Walker's home at 9:00 P.M., and then – still no one seeing him – "ran several kilometers [holding the rifle in his hands], seen by no one, and then took the bus," Marina testified. On the way home Harvey *buried the rifle* somewhere, she said Harvey told her.

None of this story was true.

In addition, Marina falsely testified not only that they'd moved to Neely Street "in January, after the new year," but that she'd seen 'Harvey's' rifle (which she said had no scope) for the first time at Neely Street, "I think that was in February," "standing up in a corner or on a shelf," that

252

she'd observed Harvey cleaning 'his' rifle "four or five times" (although no cleaning equipment or supplies were ever found), that she'd also seen 'his' rifle for "the first time in New Orleans" (making that the *second* "first time" she'd seen it), that she'd seen boxes of ammunition (both at Neely Street and in New Orleans), and that she'd stopped Harvey from killing Richard Nixon. She also "recognized" 'Harvey's' revolver and its holster. The WC believed that Harvey practiced using 'his' rifle, although he had no car and no one ever saw either Harvey or 'his' rifle. And, sure enough, Marina claimed Harvey had told her he was going out to practice with 'his' rifle.

The only rational conclusion to reach about all this is that Harvey and family *never lived at the Neely Street duplex*, which was a CIA "safe house" that just served as the backdrop for the "backyard" photo. So, not only was that photo bogus but Harvey's supposed seven week stay with Marina and June at 214 W. Neely Street and *everything* that supposedly happened there is *complete fiction*, quite likely authored by the CIA's master of disinformation, David Atlee Phillips. And if the photo is fraudulent, then everything alleged about 'Harvey's' rifle and revolver is also false and shows he was framed.

~

At police headquarters Harvey finally told Capt. Fritz, *"The only thing I am here for is because I popped a policeman on the nose* in the theatre on Jefferson Avenue, which I readily admit I did, <u>*because I was protecting myself*</u>.... I never ordered any rifle by mail order or bought any money order...for such a rifle.... I didn't own any rifle. I have not practiced or shot with a rifle since I was in the Marine Corps." No one reported him saying anything about a revolver, but there exists a photo of *Lee* with a rifle, hunting squirrels with his brother Robert.

After forty-five minutes, Fritz tossed in the towel, concluding Harvey was either "the victim of an immense and well-coordinated conspiracy," or "a psychopathic liar." Harvey was then taken through the third floor hallway, where a reporter shouted, "Did you fire that rifle?" To which Harvey replied, "I don't know what dispatches you people have been given, but I emphatically deny these charges.... I have not committed any acts of violence." Again, that language is not what a tenth grade dropout raised in New Orleans would use. It also should be noted that Harvey's 'mother' had no Southern accent either.

~

Sometime during this day Fritz told reporters that Oswald's fingerprints had not been found on the Carcano.[3]

Sunday, November 24

9:30 A.M.

Fritz started questioning Harvey again and asked about the "A. J. Hidell" ID Fritz said was found in Harvey's wallet. Harvey must have known now for certain that he was being set up, since that card hadn't been in his wallet. Postal Inspector Harry Holmes testified, "That is the only time that I recall [Oswald] kind of flared up, and he said [to Fritz], 'You know as much about it as I do.' And he showed a little anger. Really the only time that he flared up." Of course Harvey was angry – he knew that someone, probably David Atlee Phillips, had given the card to the Dallas police to frame him.

However, several detectives later talked about how well Harvey had held up during questioning, "He conducted himself...better than anyone I have ever seen during investigation." "I never saw a man that could answer questions like he did." "Oswald knew exactly when to talk and when to stop." "He was way ahead of everybody else –

he knew what he was doing and seemed very confident." "He acted like he was in charge, and, as it turned out, he probably was." Fritz wondered whether Harvey had received special training in how to deflect police questioning. Harvey undoubtedly had.

About 11:00 A.M., as Harvey was getting ready to be transferred to the county jail, Detective James Leavelle put one end of handcuffs on his left wrist, the other on Harvey's right wrist, and jokingly said to him, "Lee, if anybody shoots you, I hope they're as good a shot as you are," to which Harvey supposedly replied, "You're just being melodramatic."

They went downstairs and entered the underground garage at 11:21. A reporter shouted at Harvey, "Do you have anything to say in your defense?" Before Harvey could reply, Jack Ruby lunged out of the crowd of reporters, yelling, "You killed my president, you rat son of a bitch!" and pulled the trigger of a handgun, shooting Harvey in his left side, the bullet passing through every major organ in his abdomen and cutting through his aorta.

Why did Jack Ruby shoot Harvey? He had to. Harvey was supposed to have been killed on November 22 but wasn't. That was a *big* problem for the plotters – they couldn't have withstood an investigation and trial by any competent lawyer who defended Harvey. Ruby had to eliminate him. Ruby was the only one with easy access to police headquarters, where he knew everyone and regularly brought the cops sandwiches, including this weekend. Jack was told that if he didn't kill Harvey, the Mob would not only kill him but his brothers and sisters as well. Jack had no choice. He knew they'd do it, and he knew his own death wouldn't be pretty if he didn't carry out this hit.

After Harvey was taken to the jail office, a medical student named Beiberdorf, working in the jail that day, gave Harvey CPR, the worst thing to do for a person with a gunshot wound to the abdomen, because pushing down on the chest just pumps more blood out of the body. He kept doing CPR until the ambulance arrived, three to five minutes after Harvey was shot.

The ambulance drove Harvey to Parkland Hospital, where JFK had been taken. Beiberdorf came with him and not only continued to work on Harvey's chest but also placed an oxygen cup resuscitator over his mouth – which can be fatal to a victim with a gunshot wound to the stomach. When Harvey arrived, doctors worked feverishly to save his life. They got him stabilized briefly, but then, after immense blood loss, Harvey's heart failed and couldn't be started again. Harvey died at 1:07 P.M. at the age of 23.

Harvey's body was turned over to the Miller Funeral Home in Fort Worth. Mortician Paul Groody later reported that an FBI team with a camera and crime lab kit had come and spent a long time with the body, fingerprinting it. Groody complained, "I had a heck of a time getting the black fingerprint ink off his hands in time for burial."

FBI agent Richard Harrison later said that he and agent Vincent Drain had driven the "Oswald" rifle to the Miller Funeral Home. Harrison said he believed that Drain intended to place Oswald's palm print on the rifle "for comparison purposes."[1] Lt. Carl Day claimed he had discovered a palm print on the Carcano before turning it over to the FBI on Friday evening. However, the FBI reported on Saturday that there were no fingerprints on the Carcano.[2]

Oswald had been fingerprinted three times while alive. There has never been an explanation for why he was once again fingerprinted while dead.

Monday, November 25

4:00 P.M.

On the gloomy afternoon of this day, Harvey's body was driven for burial to a remote corner of Rose Hill Cemetery in Fort Worth. Morticians Paul Groody and Alan Baumgardner had prepared Harvey's body for burial, embalming it with several times the usual amount of formaldehyde, should Harvey's body ever be needed in the future.[1] They then had placed the body in a wood casket, which was put into a 2700 pound vault made of steel-reinforced heavy concrete with an asphalt lining – guaranteed not to break, crack, or go to pieces. The casket and vault were both hermetically sealed.

However, every church and every pastor approached had refused to conduct a service for Harvey. One minister finally agreed to come to the burial but didn't show up. Finally, the executive secretary of the Fort Worth Council of Churches said a few words.

Only Marina, June, Rachel, Robert and 'Marguerite'

259

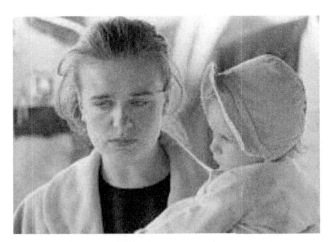

Marina and June.

attended the burial. There were no pallbearers: reporters present had to volunteer to carry the coffin. The coffin was lowered into the ground at 4:28. The whole event lasted twenty minutes.

Epilogue

Three weeks after Harvey was buried, Secret Service agents came to mortician Paul Groody and asked, "Paul, did you see any scars such as the scars on [Oswald's] wrists where he was supposed to have tried to commit suicide in Russia"? Groody said he didn't remember seeing any marks of that kind, and a Secret Service agent responded, "Well Paul, we just don't know who we have out there in that grave."[1]

In 1981 the vault was exhumed. Groody and Baumgardner were present at the exhumation and saw that the vault's bottom was now broken, although the top was still intact. However, the casket's top – just above and behind the head – also was damaged, with a section *missing*. Human remains could be seen through the large hole, but since water and air had entered over the years, only the skull and skeleton remained. The morticians next noticed the *lack of a craniotomy* – when the skull cap is cut off to remove the brain during an autopsy – *which **had** been* *done* to Harvey's head during his autopsy.

Four forensic pathologists compared the teeth in the skull with 'Lee Harvey Oswald's' Marine Corps dental records (but *which* 'Lee Harvey Oswald' records?), noted a hole caused by a mastoidectomy on the left side of the skull (but there is *no* picture of it), and concluded, "Beyond any doubt, and I mean any doubt, the individual buried under the name Lee Harvey Oswald...is in fact Lee Harvey Oswald." Apparently Lee: no craniotomy, a mastoidectomy hole and the teeth of "Lee Harvey Oswald." Either the bodies were switched or Lee and Harvey literally were merged in death – Lee's skull and Harvey's skeleton, only the heads exchanged, probably in 1964. Yet there is no missing front tooth in a photo supposedly of the skull.

Groody provided an explanation, "I feel as though someone had gone to the cemetery [during]...off hours, had taken the head of Lee Harvey Oswald, brought the vault to the surface as best they could, being a heavy item.... The vault fell, breaking [it], causing the casket to deteriorate to a degree. Then, of course, removed the head of the one that was there that had been autopsied, and put this head in its place so that we would find the teeth of Lee Harvey Oswald.... Whoever caused that is the same faction that caused the assassination in the first place. In my mind, a cover-up had taken place."

~

What about Marina? She was a twenty-two-year-old recent Russian immigrant, a widow with two babies, broke, no job and no income, who was terrified of being sent back to Russia or imprisoned here, and who was held by the FBI and Secret Service and 'interviewed' at least forty-six times in the following seventy-three days by government agents. Marina had no choice. She joined the charade and parroted the 'facts' the FBI had taught her. On February 3, 1964, she testified before the WC, lying like any CIA agent, especially about 'Harvey's' rifle and about the "backyard" photograph.

Five days later, a 'movie production company' rented a small office on the Samuel Goldwyn Studios lot in Los Angeles. The company was called Onajet Productions, also known as Tex-Italia Films and Cinema International Productions. On February 15, Marina signed a contract with Onajet and was paid a large but odd amount: $132,350– $75,000 for worldwide movie and TV rights, $7,500 for each film appearance, and $1,500 for each personal appearance. $132,350 in 1963 roughly equals $1,265,000 today.[2]

So, a 'movie production company' that has no previous

history pays Marina the equivalent of $1.265 million, never makes a film, never has Marina appear on TV or make a personal appearance, is shortly kicked off the Goldwyn lot *for not paying its office rent*, and then the Onajet 'producers' – who gave phony names – disappear and are never heard of again, without even trying to sell the rights they 'bought' from Marina.[3] Onajet is spelled C-I-A.

~

Early in '64, WC member Senator Richard Russell asked Army Intelligence Col. Phillip Corso to quietly investigate "Oswald." Corso reported back that two U.S. passports had been issued to "Lee Harvey Oswald," which had been used by two different men. Corso also discovered – from William C. Sullivan, head of the FBI's Domestic Intelligence Division – that there were two different birth certificates for "Lee Harvey Oswald," also used by two different men.[4] Russell and Corso concluded there'd been a conspiracy.

Republican Senator Richard Schweiker told researcher Anthony Summers, "...one of the biggest cover-ups in the history of our country occurred.... Oswald was playing an intelligence role.... [He was] a product of, and interacting with, the intelligence community." Summers also quoted an unnamed HSCA staff investigator, "In the months leading up to the assassination, I think Oswald got in over his head. He was no longer quite sure who he was working for, or why. Somebody was using him, and they knew exactly how and why."

Jim Garrison said, "[Oswald] was employed by the Central Intelligence Agency and was obviously drawn into a scapegoat situation and made to believe ultimately that he was penetrating the assassination. And then when the time came, they took the scapegoat – the man who thought he was working for the United States government – and killed him real quick. And then the machinery, disinformation machinery, started turning, and they started making a villain out of a man who genuinely was probably a hero." [5]

Naval Intelligence conducted an extensive investigation into the assassination and concluded that "Oswald was incapable of masterminding the assassination or of doing the actual shooting."

On March 22, 1978, James B. Wilcott, a former CIA paymaster, testified before the HSCA that he believed Harvey had been a full-time field agent for the CIA, working in the "Oswald Project," given a full-time salary for doing CIA operational work as an agent, for which project Wilcott believed he had disbursed funds in Japan.

Hunter Leake, Deputy New Orleans CIA Chief in 1963,

said that he personally paid "Oswald various sums of cash for his services." FBI clerk William Walter, who'd been in the New Orleans FBI office in 1963, told the HSCA that Harvey had "an informant's status with our office."[6]

In 1996 former Deputy Counsel for the HSCA Robert Tanenbaum testified at the *Assassination Records Review Board* (ARRB) hearing in Los Angeles that in 1964 Texas Attorney General [Waggoner Carr], Dallas District Attorney Henry Wade, and attorney Leon Jaworsky spoke to Chief Justice [Earl Warren] "and said in substance that they had information from unimpeachable sources that Lee Harvey Oswald was a contract employee of the CIA and the FBI." Warren said he'd check into that. There's no record he ever did.

George de Mohrenschildt, Harvey's first CIA 'babysitter', wrote, "The amusing and attractive side of Lee's personality was that he liked to play with his own life – he was an actor in real life…. Lee was above all an individualist, an idealist who hoped to change the world." Both George and his wife Jeanne insisted to Jim Garrison that Harvey had just been the scapegoat of the assassination.

~

George O'Toole found a recorded statement that Harvey had made in a DPD corridor:

REPORTER. Did you shoot the president?

HARVEY. I didn't shoot anybody, no sir.

O'Toole got a "former army intelligence agent and one of the most experienced polygraph examiners in the country," Lloyd H. "Rusty" Hitchcock, to run a PSE test on Harvey's statement. Hitchcock wrote, "I can state, beyond reasonable doubt, that Lee Harvey Oswald did not kill President Kennedy and did not shoot anyone else." O'Toole asked several other experts to run PSE analyses of Harvey's statement as well, and they all reached the same conclusion: Harvey was innocent.

No "lone nut," no antiquated Italian carbine, no three shots, no "magic bullet."

Just the first coup d'etat in United States history.

Conclusion

After almost sixty years, it would seem to make sense for the government to finally reveal the conspiracy that ended John Kennedy's life. But no, that will probably take another hundred years—or more. Why? Because the people of the United States already distrust government and discovering that many high level federal employees had participated in the murder of JFK could end whatever vestigial trust Americans still have in their government, which, consequently, could end American democracy.

Yet it now seems futile to keep searching for the actual participants. Everyone significant must be dead by now. Even Robert Oswald is gone, and although Marina is still alive, all she could tell us is that she had to lie.

Nevertheless, it is important to identify what *sort* of men took part in the coup and cover-up:

- high level CIA officers;
- the head of the FBI and his agents;
- high level elected government officials;

- some top brass in the Pentagon;

- Secret Service agents at all levels;

- Texas oil barons;

- anti-Castro Cuban exiles;

- private Dallas citizens, like those in the TSBD, who had certain connections;

- a number of DPD officers;

- top Mob figures;

- politically far Right individuals, who may not have participated but knew what was coming;

- and most important and totally unknown—except for brief speculation—the highest figures in civilian society: top bankers, lawyers, financiers, industrialists: the men who run the country and probably the world—of whom not a word will ever be spoken or put into print.

It is mind-boggling how many important figures lent their assent to the murder of a U.S. President, prior and/or after the coup. And before it is claimed that it was their patriotic duty, it is well to reveal their real motives, to list what these men would have lost had JFK lived:

- CIA: JFK had fired the top three officials of the CIA, had begun the process of dismantling The Company;

270

- FBI: JFK would have retired J. Edgar Hoover on his 70th birthday;
- Lyndon Johnson: was being investigated by the Justice Department, was expected to be indicted and convicted. and would not have been on the 1964 presidential ticket in any case;
- Pentagon: its brass wanted to invade Cuba, start a major war in Vietnam, even nuke Russia, all of which JFK had vetoed;
- Secret Service: some agents just hated JFK, mostly for his support of civil rights;
- Texas oil barons: JFK was planning to eliminate the oil depletion allowance, which would have cost the oil men many millions in profit;
- anti-Castro Cuban exiles: no possibility to mount another invasion of Cuba with JFK alive;
- high-level Dallas figures: greed, the old-boy network, all interconnected with the military-industrial network: no opportunity for power and profit while JFK remained president for another five years;
- the Mob: hounded mercilessly by Robert Kennedy, who was bent on destroying the entire Mob;

- DPD officers: simply part of the "old boy" network, who worked hand-in-glove with the CIA, FBI and Army Intelligence, a number of whom were members of the Klan and/or the John Birch Society;

- high level civilians: JFK's biggest sin was not waging large wars that would have generated huge profits.

Finally, there were low level figures, like FBI agents, who feared for their jobs, their families, their pensions and their lives, who could not have changed events in any case.

Ultimately, the purpose of revealing the facts dug up by thousands of citizen investigators over the past six decades has been to prevent another coup from taking place without consequences for any participants. And what *should* be revealed *now* is the real identity and function(s) of Harvey Oswald, but that also is most unlikely to happen.

At the very least, however, those who are reading this book can see that they have been lied to by their government and by all major media and who sometime in the future may decide to demand that a true account be provided of the tragedy which derailed American history and brought us to where the country is today.

We are still waging the long twilight struggle that JFK

spoke of and we still have not excised the malignancy on the spirit of the United States. Can a new generation of Americans end the moral corruption, unearth America's darkest secrets and excise the spiritual disease afflicting the United States? That is the hope. For without that cleansing, America will never reach its full potential.

Appendix

JFK 'AUTOPSY'

The wounds inflicted on JFK that were seen in Dallas by witnesses, doctors, nurses and others have been noted above, which should have closed that inquiry. However, it didn't, for what was later seen and recorded at Bethesda Naval Hospital was a horse of a very different color. David S. Lifton spent fifteen years investigating the facts of JFK's autopsy and then wrote his 747 page book *Best Evidence*, published in 1980. The information about the autopsy that follows all came from his research.

To summarize JFK's wounds, as seen in Parkland Hospital: a shot to the throat from the front, small entrance wound, no exit wound seen; a shot to the left temporal area from the front, which blew an egg-sized hole in the right lower quadrant of the back of JFK's skull; a shot to the head from the rear that passed through the egg-sized hole, no exit wound seen; an explosive bullet shot from the front, from the far west segment of the stockade fence, that hit the right temporal area and blew up a large part of JFK's brain; plus some chest injury.

What was *not* seen or found in Dallas was a much larger head wound on the right side and top; a small entrance bullet hole on the back of JFK's head just below the large wound; a shallow bullet wound in the back; and a sizable, ragged-edged wound in JFK's throat. Nor, in Dallas, were any cuts made in JFK's scalp, skull or brain, nor what remained of JFK's brain cut loose from its moorings with a scalpel.

Rather than conclude at the end of this Appendix with what apparently happened to JFK's body, what has been concluded – based on Lifton's investigations – will be given just below, followed by the facts to support the conclusion.

JFK's body was removed from its bronze casket sometime after it was placed aboard Air Force One in Dallas and before it reached Bethesda Naval Hospital. It then was taken by plane and/or helicopter to Walter Reed Army Medical Center, where it was operated on.

Four symmetrical cuts – all at about 90^0 angles from each other – were made in JFK'S scalp, four flaps of skin were peeled back and the top of the skull was sawed apart into pieces to simulate being shattered by a high velocity bullet. The brain was then cut loose from the spinal cord and removed from the cranium. Three slits were cut in the brain, front to back, in order to remove bullets or bullet fragments, which had been located with X-rays. What next happened to the brain between this operation and the start of the formal autopsy at Bethesda Naval Hospital is unknown.

The large hole in the back of JFK's head seen in Dallas was greatly enlarged (see drawings below). Two "bullet holes" were then created: one a small entrance wound below the large head wound in the rear, the other a very shallow entrance wound in JFK's back.

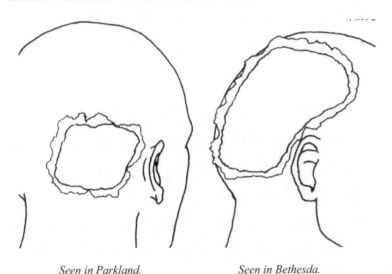

Seen in Parkland.   *Seen in Bethesda.*

The purposes of the operation were to demonstrate that; 1) the wounds all came from the rear, 2) there were only three shots, and 3) all the bullets were shot from 'Lee Harvey Oswald's rifle,' the Carcano.

The body (now naked, with a sheet wound around its head) was put in a dark military body bag, then in a cheap military metal shipping casket and flown by helicopter to an area somewhere behind Bethesda, where it was placed in a navy ambulance and brought to the rear loading dock. Subsequently, the body was taken from the shipping casket, removed from the body bag and either put back in the bronze casket or placed directly on the autopsy table.

Some of the following information is contradictory; some is – presently – inexplicable. The reader will have to decide what to believe from those facts. Page numbers of *Best Evidence* are in parentheses.

TRANSPORT OF BODY

A Bethesda technician said he heard two, perhaps three, helicopters in the distance behind Bethesda, so the body may have been brought by helicopter and then transferred to a navy ambulance. (605)

Medical personnel reported that JFK's body arrived at the loading dock in back of Bethesda in a cheap metal casket (601), brought there by a navy ambulance, not the hearse in which Jackie Kennedy was riding. Instead of the sheet with which he had left Parkland being wrapped around him and a plastic mattress cover under him, JFK was now in an ordinary dark military body bag, such as used for military casualties overseas, and was naked, a sheet wrapped around his head, probably to keep the pieces of the skull from falling apart (600-601).

The time the body arrived and the time the formal autopsy began is not at all clear. Chief autopsist Dr. James Humes noted that the body had been brought in to the autopsy room at 7:30 P.M., the military casket team put the time at 8:00 P.M. (564), and the start of the formal autopsy time was given as 10:30 P.M. To further confuse the time issue, a technician told Lifton that X-rays had already been taken (second or third trip) of JFK's body when Jackie Kennedy entered the building with the bronze casket (620). So, sometime and somewhere, the body was either put back in the bronze casket or was placed directly onto the autopsy table, when and by whom unknown.

DEVIATIONS FROM PARKLAND OBSERVATIONS

- Dr. John Ebersole: "At the base of the throat, a very neatly sutured, neatly sewed, opening that we interpreted initially as a surgical wound" (544). Appears to be an attempt to make the wound seem what it wasn't. However, the autopsy photos show a large *jagged* open hole in

279

JFK's throat.

- The wound in the side/top of JFK's head had become 8" X 4" in size (601).

- An apparent bullet wound was now seen on JFK's back, approximately 4" down from the shoulder and 2.5" to the right. Dr. Pierre Finck, Bethesda: The wound was "the first fraction of an inch" deep (281). The "magic bullet" was 1.2" long. The back wound and clothing holes did not match (281). The coat hole was 3.55 times the diameter of the bullet, the shirt hole 2.25 as large (284). This back hole did not match up with the supposed "exit" hole in JFK's throat. The "magic bullet" supposedly had fallen out of the back hole during CPR, but the hole was about half the length of the bullet and, anyhow, *how could it fall out of the hole if it entered JFK's back, exited his throat, went through Connally and into his left thigh?* Patently impossible. Absurd.

- The most provocative fact of the entire autopsy, was provided by two FBI agents, James Siebert and Francis O'Neill (97), who in the autopsy room wrote in their very detailed report that one of the autopsy doctors had said, "Surgery on the head area, namely in the top of the skull" (296).

- A 15 mm X 5 mm wound was now seen below the large wound on the right side of the head (328). David Lifton suspected this wound and the back wound were *created* at Walter Reed. They were not seen by anyone at Parkland Hospital.

SKULL ANOMALIES

- Four equally-spaced flaps of skin had been cut in the scalp, made post-mortem (437, 444).

- It was not necessary to cut off the top of the skull – pieces of skull fell to the autopsy table (602).

- The skull was shattered *on the left* cerebral hemisphere, not just the right (438).

BRAIN ANOMALIES

- Paul Kelly O'Connor, a lab technologist, told Lifton: "[JFK] didn't have any brains left – it blew all the brains out – there wasn't anything to remove – the cranium was empty – nothing was left" (542, 602). Then the cranium was filled with plaster of Paris (603).

- However, lab tech James Curtis Jenkins told Lifton that he put a brain into formaldehyde – and he believed a bullet came from the front (607, 609).

- A Bethesda doctor: the brain was removed quite easily (438).

- The brain came out without being cut free (454). Apparently the brain was removed before the autopsy, in order to take out bullets and/or bullet fragments from it.

- There were three cuts (lacerations) in the brain, front to back, one 2" deep that ran the length of the brain (174), one *on the left* side, on the underside of the brain, *no exit wound* (251). These cuts seem to have been *made* to remove bullets or bullet fragments. The cuts did not seem to have been made by bullets, as the cuts were quite clean.

BULETS AND FRAGMENTS

- FBI agents Siebert and O'Neill reported that "doctors were at a loss to explain why they could find no bullets in JFK's body" (175, 282).

- Admiral David P. Osborne, Chief of Surgery at Bethesda, said that at the start of the autopsy he saw an intact bullet roll onto the autopsy table (590). "I had that bullet in my hand and looked at it.... The bullet was not deformed in any way." Several others held it, including a Secret Service agent. "It fell out on the autopsy table" (646). The "magic bullet" again?

- There is a receipt, executed by FBI agents Siebert and O'Neill, made out to Capt. J. H. Stover, "We hereby acknowledge the receipt of a missel [sic] removed by Commander James J. Humes, MC, USN on this date" (590).

- A memo was typed up by Petty Officer Dennis David at the direction of a Secret Service agent, that "four large pieces of lead were removed" during the autopsy (578).

- Two large fragments, the nose and tail parts of bullets, supposedly were found in JFK's limousine, in the front, claimed to be from the shot that struck JFK in the head (185). (However, it has been reported elsewhere that a medical corpsman, Thomas Mills, found, in the White House garage that night, a *whole* bullet on the floor in the *rear* of the limousine. The bullet was jacketed, straight but with a bent tip. Also found were three pieces of skull.)[1]

SWORN TO SILENCE

All personnel associated in any way with the body or autopsy were sworn to secrecy – they could lose their pensions, be court-martialed, not be promoted, etc. if they talked. This order was not rescinded for ten years, during which time no one would talk.

CONCLUSION

JFK's autopsy was not an ordinary, normal one. This author agrees with David Lifton that there was a pre-autopsy manipulation of JFK's body, attempting to conform the body to the plotters' chosen scenario of "a lone nut" killing JFK, using a Carcano carbine, shooting three times from the sixth floor "sniper's nest" in the Texas School Book Depository building, behind JFK.

That – as has been shown – is not what happened. In 1982 Admiral George Burkley, M.D. told a researcher that he believed Kennedy's death was the result of a conspiracy.[2]

~

SIX KILLERS' FATES

Johnny Roselli was brutally murdered, asphyxiated, on August 7, 1976, in Miami, by some of his associates.

Lucien Sarti was shot to death in April, 1972, in

Mexico City by Mexican federal police, during a raid on a drug trafficking ring.

Lee Oswald disappeared soon after the event, likely was 'eliminated.'

"Mac" Wallace died on January 7, 1971, when, oddly, his car hit a bridge abutment and ran off the road near Pittsburgh, Texas.

James Files was given a fifty-year sentence for attempted murder of two police officers in 1991. He was paroled in 2016 and is still living. He confessed to killing JFK.

Frank Sturgis, one of the Watergate 'plumbers,' was convicted and served fourteen months in prison. He worked for the CIA for many years, before and after JFK's assassination, was a member of Operation 40—trained as an assassin to kill Castro by the CIA, bragged to Marita Lorenz that he had participated in JFK's murder. He died on December 4, 1993 of cancer.

Notes

Introduction

1. Schwimmer, p. 330, Note 15.
2. Armstrong, *Harvey & Lee*, p. 206.
3. Marrs, p. xvii.
4. Hereafter 'Harvey' will be shown simply as Harvey.

Prelude

1. Palamara, *Honest Answers*, pp. 51-55.
2. Turner, The Forces of Darkness, *The Men Who Killed Kennedy.*
3. Dankbar.
4. Spartacus Educational, *Operation 40.*
5. Lorenz, p. 131, also her HSCA testimony.
6. *Ibid.,* p. 131.
7. Arnes.
8. Benson, p. 472.
9. *Mysteries of the 112th Intelligence Group.*
10. Elliott, p. 23.
11. The times shown in this volume cannot be verified to the minute, but they are as accurate as possible.
12. Baker, p. 504.
13. prayer-man, <u>*Bill Shelley.*</u>
14. *Ibid., <u>Billy Lovelady</u>.*
15. Weston.
16. Spartacus Educational, <u>*David Harold Byrd.*</u>
17. *Ibid.*
18. Palamara, *Honest Answers*, p. 217.

19. Statement of Mary Dowling to the FBI. *See also* Car #10 – Where Are You?

20. Plumlee.

21. Davis, p. 123.

22. Since Wesley Frazier also said that "Oswald" had curtain rods, the curtain rods story seems to be a deliberate fabrication.

23. Was that photo the infamous "backyard photo" of Oswald?

24. Armstrong, *Harvey & Lee*, p. 781.

25. *Ibid.*, p. 729.

26. Baker, *Me & Lee*, p. 519.

27. *Ibid.*, p. 505.

28. *Ibid.*, p. 519.

29. *Ibid.*, p. 521.

30. Baker, *Me & Lee*, p. 536 (8).

31. Lorenz, pp.131-136, also Lane, pp. 296-297.

32. Stone, pp. 226 - 227.

Friday, November 22

1. Palamara, *Survivor's Guilt*, pp. 150-151.

2. Statement to the FBI. *See also* Car #10 – Where Are You?

3. Plumlee.

4. It seems significant that Harvey removed the symbol of the husband (wedding ring) and slipped on the symbol of the warrior (Marine Corps ring).

5. Question: why was Harvey wearing such shabby clothes, when he had $185, was getting $200 a month from the FBI and $200 a month from the CIA? Answer: an intelligence operative is not permitted to live above his job income – it would raise questions as to where his money came from and soon blow his "cover."

5a. This account has been strongly questioned by Larry Rivera in his book *The JFK Horsemen*.

6. Marrs, p.41.

7. Armstrong, *Harvey, Lee and Tippit*.

8. All material above is from WC testimony.

9. Douglas, p. 271.

10. Plumlee.

11. Shaw, p. 10, and Douglas, p. 255.

12. Palamara, *Survivor's Guilt.*

13. *Ibid.,* pp. 138-142.

14. Vaughan.

15. Sneed, p. 458.

16. Palamara, *Honest Answers,* p. 216.

17. Douglas, p. 285.

18. Weston, *Kennedys and King.*

19. Marrs, p. 26.

20. Several people called the sixth floor the fifth floor, apparently because what they noticed was the fifth row of windows up on the building.

21. Lifton, P. 29.

22. Marrs, pp. 77-79.

23. FBI Report, *Evelyn Harris.*

24. Eaves.

25. Marrs, p. 44.

26. Elliott, p. 21.

27. Lewis.

28. Sneed, p. 71.

29. *Ibid.*, p.86.

30. Lane, p. 303.

31. Fetzer, pp. 152-153.

32. Some claim that "Badge Man" was Dallas policeman Roscoe White, who was seen on the grassy knoll by Beverly Oliver without his hat or side arm, but if it was him, where did his rifle go? And how was *he* recruited and by whom? He really does not fit into the known facts.

33. Palamara, *Honest Answers*, p. 333.

34. Benson, p. 107.

35. Sneed, p. 96.

36. Marrs, p.16.

37. Palamara, *Honest Answers*, p. 178.

38. Palamara, *Honest Answers.*

39. Marrs, p. 30.

40. Baker.

41. Palamara, *Honest Answers*, p. 323.

42. Marrs, p. 44.

43. Spartacus Educational, *John Connally*.

44. Palamara, *Honest Answers*, p. 306

45. *Ibid.* p. 321.

46. Sneed, p. 145.

47. *Ibid.*, p. 147.

48. Morrison.

49. *The Men Who Killed Kennedy.*

50. Palamara, *Honest Answers*, p. 183.

51. Sneed, p. 82.

52. *SundayMirror.*

53. Palamara, *Honest Answers*, p.47.

54. *Ibid.,* pp. 34-35.

55. *Ibid.*

56. *Ibid.*

57. The only shot Files fired. He was told by David Atlee Phillips to fire only if Files saw JFK was still alive.

58. Ernest, p.83.

59. Fetzer, p. 133.

60. Ernest, pp. 78, 82, 121.

61. Marrs, p. 307.

62. Douglas, p. 264; Marrs, pp. 83-84.

63. Benson, p. 30.

64. Marrs, pp. 37-38.

65. *Ibid,.* pp. 313-14.

66. Marrs, pp. 223, 453, 456-7.

67. Lifton, p. 29.

68. Marrs, pp. 80-81.

69. *Ibid.*, p.24

70.. Douglas, pp. 262-63; Marrs, pp. 79-80.

71. Marrs, p. 24.

72. Ernest, p. 61.

73. Ernest.

74. Prayer Man, *Peggy Joyce Hawkins.*

75. Truly.

76. Jarman.

77. Email from Sandra Styles to Sean Murphy, dated 4/29/2011, "[Vicki] also told office workers that on the way down she noticed the freight elevator cables were moving." No telling in which direction. Vicki could only have seen the west cables, next to the stairs. This places the elevator moving between 20 to 70 seconds after the last shot. The elevator took about 30 seconds to go from the 6th to the 1st floor, meaning the killers exited the TSBD only 30-60 seconds behind Vicki.

78. One of the more perplexing things about the whereabouts of "Lee Harvey Oswald" between noon and 12:33 P.M. on November 22 is the Coke bottle "Oswald" is reported to have had. At 11:50 A.M. Harvey was seen on the first floor by Bill Shelley. At noon, Harvey told Eddie Piper that he was going upstairs to eat in the second floor lunchroom. At 12:15, or slightly later, Harvey was seen in the lunchroom by Carolyn Arnold. Just before 12:33, "Oswald" was *supposedly* seen in the lunchroom by police officer Marion L. Baker, who testified that he first saw "Oswald" walking away from him in the lunchroom toward the east end of the room, about *twenty feet* from him. (Since the lunchroom was thirty feet long, and the Coke machine was fifteen feet from the west door, where would "Oswald" have been going, having walked past the Coke machine, after just entering the room from the west door?)

Curiously, Baker's handwritten report to the FBI on November 23 had the words "drinking a Coke" crossed out. The question then becomes, "*Why* was the Coke first included, and why was it then crossed off?" And *when* was it crossed off, and by *whom*? And Baker later testified to the Warren Commission that he did not see anything in Oswald's hands, and he did not mention a Coke. However, seconds after Baker left the lunchroom, "Oswald" (Lee) was seen by Mrs. Robert A. Reid coming out of the south door of the lunchroom, with a full bottle of Coke in his right hand, wearing a white T-shirt, not the light brown jacket that Baker claimed he saw on "Oswald."

Let's consider this for a moment. Harvey goes up to eat his lunch (a cheese sandwich and an apple) at noon, is seen eating his lunch at 12:15. Yet he supposedly does not buy a Coke until about 12:33. How many people would eat a whole dry sandwich without anything to drink, supposedly be seen *without* a Coke in his hand, and then seconds later come out of the lunchroom *with* a full bottle of Coke in his hand? Apparently still not having drunk *any* of the Coke.

What all this means is that the scenario crafted by the CIA plotters was that Harvey would go to eat in the lunchroom to establish that fact, would leave sometime between 12:20 and 12:25 (unseen, since everyone was watching for the parade to pass by), and then would be replaced in the lunchroom at 12:33 by Lee, who would quickly buy a Coke and then walk through the secretarial area where Mrs. Reid met him – the hypothesis being that Lee would be mistaken for Harvey if anyone noticed him, which is exactly what happened. Conclusion: Baker lied – he was never in the lunchroom. (Marrs, pp. 52-53)

79. Note that Lee *knew where* to buy the Coke, knew how to get to the front stairs, knew how to get out of the building. His exit had been carefully choreographed ahead of time.

80. CE 1381.

81. Otherwise, why didn't Lee just go out the back door with the other three assassins?

82. Schmidt, *Pierce M. Allman*.

83. The Education Forum, *Robert MacNeil*.

84. FBI Report, *Evelyn Harris*.

85. Deep Politics Forum.

86. Marrs, pp. 309-11.

87. Sneed, p.519.

88. Lifton, *pp.* 59, 275.

89. *Ibid.*, p. 46.

90. *Ibid.*, p. 45.

91. *Ibid.*, p. 329.

92. Shaw, p. 71.

93. Lifton, p. 45.

94. Benson, p. 202.

95. Palamara, *Honest Answers*, p. 49.

96.*Ibid.*, p. 338.

97.*Ibid.*, p. 343.

98.*Ibid.*, p. 338.

99.*Ibid.*, p. 344.

99a. Rivera, p. 523.

100. Shaw, p. 71

101. Lifton*, pp.* 49-50.

102. *Ibid.*, p. 43.

103. *Ibid.*, p. 44.

104. *Ibid.*

105. *Ibid.*, p. 330.

106. *Ibid.*, p. 44.

106a. Rivera, p. 519.

106b. *Ibid.,* p. 417.

107. Benson, p. 139.

107a. Phillips.

108. Gilbride, p. 96.

109. Lifton, p. 317.

110. *Ibid.*, p. 279.

111. *Ibid.*, p. 280.

112. Benson, p. 218.

113. Lifton, p. 192.

114. Shaw, 71.

115. Lifton, p. 283.

116. *Ibid.*, p. 8.

117. Benson, p. 254.

118. Gilbride, p. 266.

119. Fleming and Jendro.

120. The reader is directed to the online copies of WC testimonies, an invaluable resource (See Internet Sources below).

121. Drenas, *Car #10....*

122. Lee putting a bullet in Tippit's head indicates that this was not an unplanned shooting. Tippit needed to be dead for some reason.

123. Marrs, p. 334.

124. From testimonies of WC witnesses.

125. Roberts, p. 65. The film was shot by Dallas Cinema Associates.

126. Spartacus Educational. *Thayer Waldo*.

127. Sneed, p. 233.

128. Palamara, *Honest Answers*, p. 181.

129. Armstrong, *Oswald Did Not Purchase A Rifle From Klein's.*

130. *Ibid.*

131. Marrs, pp. 422-23.

132. No gun dealer would sell a rifle in such a condition, and no customer would accept such a rifle. The rifle was also described as "crudely made, poorly designed, dangerous and inaccurate" (Shaw, p. 3). In addition, both the bolt and trigger frequently stuck, and the scope was mounted for a left-handed person.

133. Armstrong, *Harvey & Lee*, pp. 835-837.

134. One odd aspect of virtually every book written about the assassination and Lee Harvey Oswald is the seeming uncritical acceptance by authors that everything said or written by policemen, detectives, FBI agents, district attorneys, TSBD employees, and – yes, Harvey Oswald – was true.

The fact is that most male TSBD employees lied, probably a dozen detectives and policemen lied, and since there was no tape recorder or stenographer present when Harvey was interrogated for twelve hours, there is no way to determine whether any statement attributed to Harvey and reported out of Fritz's interrogation room was correct or truthful or was ever said. Anything could have been laid on Harvey after his death – and likely was.

For example, Harvey's supposed statement during interrogation that he ate his lunch in the first floor domino room, which no one corroborated, versus Harvey telling a co-worker at noon that he was going *up* to eat his lunch, plus two witnesses who said they saw Harvey in the second floor break room between 12:00 and 12:25.

The apparent myopia of researchers is due to their frame of reference. Few are willing to accept that there were two 'Oswalds', and those who believe Harvey was an ONI/CIA deep cover operative and FBI informant usually brush aside the concept of two 'Oswalds', as if this was of little significance.

It must be stressed, however, that Harvey had to be a successful lifelong liar in order to be a deep cover intelligence agent, especially this one, as he began lying – to create his new identity – when he was eleven. So, he was a very practiced liar, and it is unlikely that anyone ever caught him in his intelligence lies. He undoubtedly told some lies to Fritz. But what and why?

The answer may be that Harvey was briefed ahead of the assassination by his CIA handlers to give certain answers to certain questions related to where he was and what he was doing from about 12:15 to about 12:33. It is very obvious that the movements of Lee and the other three assassins had been choreographed ahead of time, especially Lee's movements and activities, such as buying a Coke.

All things taken into consideration, Harvey must have known exactly who Lee was and what he would do after the shooting. So Harvey may very well have been just as instructed as Lee. Consequently, Harvey likely knew that Lee would go and buy a Coke, walk down the front stairs, leave the Coke bottle in the storeroom, and walk out the front door and therefore could describe Lee's actions as if they were his own. Such lies would make it even more likely that Fritz and others would accept that Lee's actions were Harvey's. This was part of the scrambled doppelgänger scenario played out after noon in the TSBD to make witnesses think Lee was Harvey.

Bottom line: everyone lied, including Harvey, who lied like the CIA expert he was. Whatever was or was not attributed to Harvey in interrogation, nothing can be unthinkingly accepted as truth. Even Fritz and others in the interrogation room commented on Harvey's verbal skills and coolness.

So this Dallas weekend was a dance of liars.

135. From John Armstrong's article that appeared in a 1998 issue of PROBE.

136. Penn Jones Jr., in an August 26, 1971 editorial of *The Midlothian Mirror*, wrote, "Unrecorded...is the fact that a close friend to Jack Ruby, Tommy Rowe, worked at the [Hardy] shoe store [with Brewer]. Rowe told relatives that he, not Brewer, pointed out Oswald [to police]. Rowe was so close to Ruby that he moved into Ruby's South Ewing apartment when Ruby went to jail." Rowe had been living in an apartment next to Ruby's. If Rowe's story is true, then everything Brewer said was a lie. An even bigger question mark is Rowe knowing Ruby. Rowe was never interviewed by the DPD or FBI. Even stranger, witness of Oswald's arrest George Jefferson Applin, Jr. has said he saw Jack Ruby sitting in the back row of the theatre watching Oswald's arrest. And if neither Brewer nor Rowe actually saw Harvey at the shoe store, how did they know that Harvey had on a brown shirt that was hanging out of his pants? Had Harvey been instructed to wear that shirt by his handler?

137. Douglas, p. 291.

138. *Ibid.*, p. 292.

139. Gilbride, p. 283.

140. Marrs, pp. 316, 357.

141. Manchester, pp. 292-3.

142. Palamara, *Honest Answers*, p. 32.

143. Meagher, *Accessories....*, Chapter 6.

144. The likely scenario about the wallet is that Captain Westbrook brought it to the murder scene, with a bogus Selective Service ID of 'Alek James Hidell' and an 'Oswald' Uniformed Services ID (with a bogus 'Oswald' photo) in it. When Westbrook learned that 'Lee Harvey Oswald' was in the Texas Theatre, he went there with the expectation that 'Oswald' would be shot dead, at which time Westbrook would have pulled out the wallet and announced that 'Oswald' had killed

Tippit and – later – that he'd killed JFK. When Harvey was not killed at the theatre, and had a wallet, Westbrook held on to the wallet he had and later passed on the two fake IDs to associates, who then claimed the IDs were found in the wallet taken from Harvey. All this indicates that Tippit was set up for his murder.

145. All information about VSA analyses come from O'Toole's book.

146. An eighteen year study, published in 2013, found that VSA technology can identify emotional stress and detect lies better than a polygraph – it's 95% accurate.

147. Principal source for Oswald at police headquarters is Gillon.

148. #11378 G, 11/30/63.

149. CE #1146, 12/10/63.

150. Douglas, p. 365.

151. Eventually, researcher Sherman Skolnick got hold of a photocopy of the phone slip.

152. Marrs, p. 347.

153. It later was determined that Oswald had never been legally arraigned for the murder of JFK.

154. Schmidt, *Buell Wesley Frazier.*

Saturday, November 23

1. Benson, p. 132.

2. Mahlon Tobias' WC testimony is highly suspect. He said Harvey was asked to vacate his apartment for drinking and beating Marina regularly. First, Harvey was known to never drink – even Marina testified he did not drink, not even beer. Second, there was no prior record of Harvey being a violent man – this 'violence' seems to have been added to expand the Oswald 'legend.' Third, Tobias said that the owner of the property and his wife came over one night and told Harvey he would have to either stop or leave, and Harvey supposedly moved two days later, leaving behind a $5 deposit – none of which makes any sense. So, why weren't the owners called to testify? And if the Oswalds did not live on Neely Street, which they didn't, it must be deduced that Tobias lied about them leaving on March 3 – that the Oswalds continued to live at 604 Elsbeth Street after that date. Dallas Power and Light added another layer to this, when it showed (CE 1160) that Harvey's account with it at Elsbeth Street was not terminated on March 3 and electricity was used at his apartment through April 23, (supposedly Harvey's last full day at Neely Street):

     Date   Kilowatt Hours

11/3/62 – Cut-in date
12/18   182
1/18/63   84
2/19   88
3/20   54
4/19   44
4/23   16   (Final bill)

There is, however, <u>no record</u> of any electricity or gas being used by the Oswalds at 214 W. Neely Street. A meter reader came by on March 20 and reported the premises <u>vacant</u>. Dallas Power & Light received no payment for electrical services at that apartment between Jan 16 and May 2 (CE 1160). By the way, I've run across no mention of the Neely Street apartment being furnished.

3. Lifton, p. 354.

Sunday, November 24

1. Marrs, pp. 422-23.

2. *Ibid.*

Monday, November 25

1. Marrs, p. 527, and *The Men Who Killed Kennedy.*

Epilogue

1. *The Men Who Killed Kennedy.*

2. It has been reported that Marina also received a $25,000 'advance' from *Life* magazine for a book that was never written and $70,000 in donations from well-wishers. Further, Don Roberdeau has written that "A. C. Greener, the editor of the *Dallas Times Herald* newspaper's 'People's Forum' column during 1963 and 1964, has stated for the record that the *DMN* received $241,000 from readers in donations for Marina." However, this could not be verified.

3. One researcher claims that two of the "producers" were real, but no one spends that kind of money and then makes no effort to recoup it, nor abruptly leaves without paying the rent after being there just a few weeks. Marina never performed any service for this company.

4. Armstrong, p. 362.

5. *The Men Who Killed Kennedy.*

6. Douglas, p. 362.

Appendix

1. Palamara, *Honest Answers*, pp. 99, 101.

2. Marrs, p. 362.

Sources

Books

*Armstrong, John. <u>Harvey And Lee: How The CIA Framed Oswald</u>. 2003.
*Baker, Judyth Vary. <u>Me & Lee</u>. 2011.
_____. <u>David Ferrie</u>. 2014.
Belzer, Richard and Wayne, David. <u>Hit List</u>. 2013.
*Benson, Michael. <u>Who's Who In The JFK Assassination</u>. 1993, 2003.
Bishop, Jim. <u>The Day Kennedy Was Shot</u>. 1968.
*Davis, John H. <u>Mafia Kingfish</u>. 1989.
DiEugenio, J. (ed.) and Pease, L. (ed.). <u>The Assassinations</u>. 2003.
*Douglas, James W. <u>JFK And The Unspeakable</u>. 2010.
*Elliott, Todd C. <u>A Rose by Many Other Names</u>. 2013
*Ernest, Barry. <u>The Girl On The Stairs</u>. 2013.
Fetzer, James H. <u>Murder In Dealey Plaza</u>. 2000.
Fonzi, Gaeton. <u>The Last Investigation</u>. 2013.
Garrison, Jim. <u>On The Trail Of The Assassins</u>. 1991.
*Gilbride, Richard. <u>Matrix For Assassination</u>. 2009.
*Gillon, Steven M. <u>Lee Harvey Oswald: 48 Hours To Live</u>. 2013.
Groden, Robert J. <u>The Search For Lee Harvey Oswald</u>. 1995.
Groden, R. J. and Livingstone, H. E. <u>High Treason</u>. 1989.
Harris, Patrick. <u>See No Evil</u>. 2014.
Haslam, Edward T. <u>Dr. Mary's Monkey</u>. 2014.
Hepburn, J., Turner, W. <u>Farewell America: The Plot To Kill JFK</u>. 2002.
Janney, Peter. <u>Mary's Mosaic</u>. 2013.
Kantor, Seth. <u>The Ruby Coverup</u>. 1980.
*Kross, Peter. <u>American Conspiracy Files</u>. 2015.

299

*Lane, Mark. *Plausible Denial*. 1991.

Livingstone, Harrison Edward. *High Treason 2*. 1992.

*Lorenz, Marita, with Ted Schwarz. *Marita*. 1993.

*Marrs, Jim. *Crossfire: The Plot That Killed Kennedy*. 2013.

McBride, Joseph. *Into The Nightmare*. 2013.

Meagher, Sylvia. *Subject Index To The Warren Report and Hearings & Exhibits*. 1966.

*_____. *Accessories After The Fact*. 1967, 2013.

Melanson, Philip H. *Spy Saga: Lee Harvey Oswald And U.S. Intelligence*. 1990.

Morley, Jefferson. *Our Man In Mexico*. 2008.

Morris, W.R. & Cutler, R.B. *Alias Oswald*. 1985.

Newman, John. *Oswald And The CIA*. 2008.

Oliver, B., with Buchanan, C. *Nightmare In Dallas*. 1994.

Oswald, Robert L. *Lee*. 1967.

*O'Toole, George. *The Assassination Tapes*. 1975.

*Palamara, Vincent Michael. *Survivor's Guilt*. 2013.

*_____. *Honest Answers*. *2021*.

* Phillips, Donald T,, *A Deeper, Darker Truth*. 2009.

*Rivera, Larry. *The JFK Horsemen*. 2018

Roberts, Craig. *Kill Zone*. 2014.

Roberts, Craig, with Armstrong, John. *JFK: The Dead Witnesses*. 2014.

Russell, Dick. *The Man Who Knew Too Much*. 1992.

_____. *On The Trail Of The JFK Assassins*. 2008.

*Schwimmer, George. Doppelgänger: The Legend of Lee Harvey Oswald, Sixth Edition, 2022.

*Scott, Peter Dale. *Deep Politics....* 1996.

*Shaw, Gary. *Cover-up*. 1992.

Smith, Matthew. *JFK: The Second Plot*. 2002.

_____. *Say Goodbye To America*. 2005.

*Sneed, Larry A. *No More Silence*. 2017.

*Stone, R., with Colapietro, M. *The Man Who Killed Kennedy*. 2013.

*Summers, Anthony. *Conspiracy*. 1980.

Twyman, Noel H. *Bloody Treason*. 2010.

*Warren Commission. Testimonies & Exhibits. 1964.

Weberman, A. J. and Canfield, M.. *Coup d'Etat In America*. 1992.

Weisberg, Harold. *Whitewash*. 2013.

_____. *Whitewash II*. 2013.

_____. *Whitewash III*. 2013.

Internet

Abrams, Malcolm. *JFK Murder Hatched In Ruby Club*.

*Altgens, James. *Altgens6 Photograph*.

*Arnes, Michael. *Esquire, This Man Is Positive..., November 22, 2013*.

Armstrong, John. *Comrade Harvey & Agent Lee*.

_____. *Harvey And Lee*.

_____. *Harvey & Lee: How The CIA Framed Oswald*.

_____. *Harvey & Lee Home Page*.

_____. *Harvey, Lee And Tippit*.

_____. *Jack Ruby*.

_____. *Just The Facts Please*.

_____. *Manipulated, Fabricated, Disappearing Evidence*.

_____. *Marines To Minsk*.

_____. *November In Dallas.1997*.

_____. *November 22, 1963*.

* _____. *Oswald Did Not Purchase A Pistol From Seaport*.

* _____. *Oswald Did Not Purchase A Rifle From Klein's*.

_____. *The Early Lives Of Harvey And Lee*.

_____. *The Pre-Arranged Murder Of Officer Tippit*.

_____. *University Of Minnesota Speech*.

Assassination Research. *November 22, 1963*.

Bailey, George W. *Allen Dulles And The Doppelgängers*.

_____. *Lee H. Oswald's Name Missing From SSDI*.

*Baker, Russ. JFK Umbrella Man—More Doubts.

*Benson, Randolph. *JFK, Oswald, And The Raleigh Connection*.

Biffle, Kent. *This Couldn't Be Happening*.

Bisaro, Anna. *Oswald Got 'Very, Very Lucky.'*

Brussell, Mae. *The Last Words Of Lee Harvey Oswald*.

Cinque, Ralph, with Fetzer, Jim. *JFK: 49 Years In The Offing*.

Cochran, Mike. *I Was A Pallbearer....*

Craig, John S. *The Guns Of Dealey Plaza*.

*Craig, Roger. *When They Kill A President*.

*Deep Politics Forum. *JFK Assassination*.

D. C. Police Department. *Mauser*.

Drenas, Bill. *An Overlooked Texas Theatre Witness*.

*_____. Car #10 Where Are You?

_____. *The Top Ten Record Shop*.

*Eaves, Richard. An Eye Witness in Dealey Plaza.

Ericson, Greg. *48th JFK Anniversary*.

*FBI Report. *Evelyn Harris*.

Fetzer, James H., with Baker, Judyth Vary. *JFK: Judyth Vary Baker Cements Oswald In The Doorway*.

*Files, James E. *Confession Of James E. Files.*

Fleming, Trish and Jendro, Zach. *The Curious Case Of The American Bakeries Pay Voucher*.

*Fritz, J. W. *Report Of Interrogation Of Lee Harvey Oswald*.

*George, M. Waldo. *Affidavit.*

Gilbride, Richard. *William Shelley – Betrayal And Perjury*.

_____. *Inside Job.*

Golz, Earl. *Was Oswald In Window?*

Hewett, Carol. *Silencers, Sniper Rifles, & The CIA*.

History Matters. *Oswald, The CIA, And Mexico City*.

_____. *Jack Hammond, CE 3001*.

Hooke, Richard, with Fetzer, Jim. *Oswald Wasn't Even A Shooter*.

_____. *Bill Shelley's Shrunken Head*.

Hopsicker, Daniel. *Barry Seal, The CIA Camp In Lacombe....*

*Jarman, James. CO-2-34030, 12/7/63, P 11.

jfk1963. *Acme Building Maintenance*.

JFKCalc. *Dealey Plaza: Witness Surveys*.

JFK Facts. *Greg Parker.*

JFK Lancer. *Ruth And Michael Paine*.

Jones, Penn, Jr. *Forgive My Grief II*.

_____. *Forgive My Grief: v. 1-4*.

*Lewis, Roy Edward. *Prayer Man*.

Mary Ferrell Foundation.

*media.nara.gov. *William Shelley*.

*Morrison, James. *Quora*,

Morrow, Robert. *The LBJ-CIA Assassination Of JFK*.

Myers, Dale K. *Oswald's Mail-Order Revolver Purchase*.

National Archives: JFK Assassination Records: *JFK Key Persons.*

Orchard, William. *The Shots In Dealey Plaza.*

Oswald Innocence Campaign. *The Likeness Of Oswald And Doorman*.

Oswald TSBD Application Form.

Parker, Greg. *Neely Street Questions, Page 2.*

Palamara, Vince. *On Security And Secret Service*.

Parnell, W. Tracy. *The Exhumation Of Lee Harvey Oswald*.

*Plumlee, Robert "Tosh". *Declaration*, also *Tosh*.

*prayer-man.com. *Bill Shelley*.

*_____, *Billy Lovelady*.

*_____, *Peggy Joyce Hawkins*.

*Proctor, Grover B., Jr. *The Raleigh Call*.

Prouty, Fletcher. *The Guns Of Dallas*.

Reitzes, David. *Constructing The Assassin, Part 4*.

Reopen Kennedy Case. *Jack Edwin Dougherty*.

Rivera, Larry, with Fetzer, Jim. *JFK: Why Buell Wesley Frazier Was Erased From Altgens6*.

Rivera, Larry, and Schaeffer, Roy: *The James "Ike" Altgens JFK Photo Timeline*.

Roberts, Earlene. *Affidavit*.

Rohde, Dusty. *The Murder of J. D. Tippit*.

Russell, Dick. *Oswald And The CIA*.

*Schmidt, Markus. *Pierce M. Allman*.

*_____. *Buell Wesley Frazier*.

* Spartacus Educational, *David Harold Byrd*.

*_____, *Operation 40*.

*_____, *John Connally*.

*_Sunday Mirror_ (U.K), *November 10, 2013*.

Texas State Library Archives, Attorney General's Office.

The National Archives Catalog. *George, M. Waldo*.

*Truly, Roy S. DPD affidavit, Nov. 23, 1963.

United States Federal Census, 1940. *Emil Kardos*.

Vaughan, T.W. *Presidential Motorcade Listing*. 1993.

Warren Commission. *Guide To Numbered Exhibits*.

Warren Commission. *List Of Exhibits*.

*_____. *JFK Assassination Witness Page*.

_____. Exhibit 162.

_____. *Exhibit 369- detail*.

_____.Exhibit 1150.

*_____. *CE 1381*.

WDSU. *Transcript Of FPCC Debate*.

Wernerhoff, Carl. *The Neely Street Mysteries*.

Weston, William. *The Spider's Web: The Texas School Book Depository And The Dallas Conspiracy*.

*_____. *Kennedys and King: The CIA and the Texas School Book Depository*, April 16, 2020.

_____. *The Glaze Letters*.

_____. *411 Elm Street*.

*Wikipedia. *Voice Stress Analysis*.

Wilcott, James. *Testimony*.

Yusuf, Gokay Hasan. *Gerald Hill And The Murder Of Officer Tippit - Part 1*.

_____. *Gerald Hill And The Murder Of Officer Tippit – Part 2*.

_____. *Gerald Hill And The Framing Of Lee Harvey Oswald*.

DVDs

*Dankbaar, Wim. *Confessions From The Grassy Knoll*, 2013.

*Turner, Nigel. *The Men Who Killed Kennedy*, 1991,

Newspapers

*New York Herald Tribune, November 23, 1963.

*The Dallas Morning News, November 23, 1963.

*All titles were consulted, the starred ones cited.

Printed in Great Britain
by Amazon

38617792R00175